# HOW TO SPEAK DOG!

A Marshall Edition
Conceived, edited, and designed by Marshall Editions
The Old Brewery
6 Blundell Street
London N7 9BH

All rights reserved. Published by Scholastic Inc.

SCHOLASTIC, SCHOLASTIC REFERENCE, and associated logos are
trademarks and/or registered trademarks of Scholastic Inc.

ISBN-10: 0-545-02078-6
ISBN-13: 978-0-545-02078-7

Publisher: Richard Green
Commissioning editor: Claudia Martin
Photography: John Daniels
Art direction: Sarah Robson
Project editor: Amy Head
Layout and design: Alec Chin
Indexer: Thea Lenarduzzi
Production: Nikki Ingram

Printed and bound in China by 1010 Printing International Limited.

10 9 8 7 6 5 4 3 2 1

First printing, January 2008

# HOW TO SPEAK DOG!

**By Sarah Whitehead**

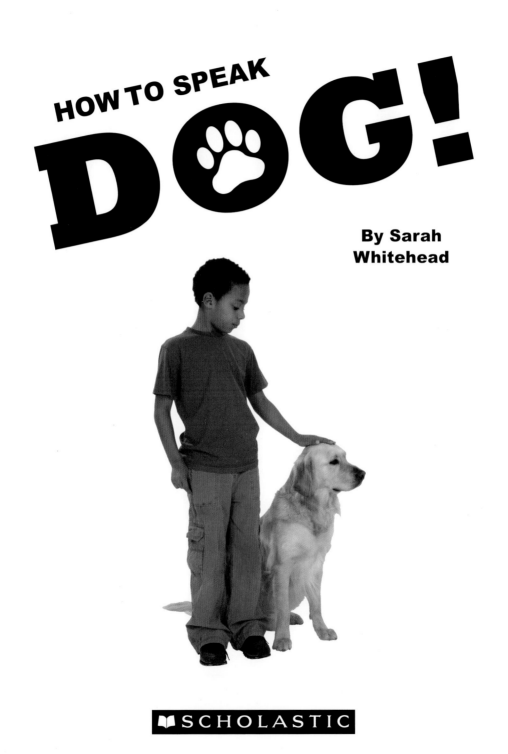

SCHOLASTIC

# Contents

# Introduction

**Our dogs are not just pets—they are members of our families. Getting to know and understand your dog will mean that you can communicate with each other, and develop a unique bond.**

Communicating with your dog is easy, when you know how! Just like learning any new language, it is important to be patient and take time to understand that there are many differences, as well as some similarities, between our languages. Dogs may not use words to express themselves, but they have many other ways to demonstrate their feelings and intentions. Learning what each of your dog's body postures and facial expressions mean is an exciting journey into the life of a completely different species, while learning how to respond to them means that your relationship will flourish.

Although all dogs share basic canine characteristics, there are huge differences between different breeds, types, and even individuals. Like a person does, each dog has their own character, likes and dislikes, and needs. It's up to us to make sure we know what these are.

**Each dog has their own character, likes and dislikes, and needs.**

**When they bark, dogs are communicating. Humans might yell instead!**

Of course, in order to live with us, dogs need to learn how to behave and how to communicate with humans, too. Just like us, dogs need to learn how to be polite and how to fit in with a routine and way of life. Training your dog should not be a battle of wills or a chore, but should be fun and enjoyable for both of you. Understanding what your dog is "saying" will make this process much easier and more rewarding. Your dog will be happy to spend time with you and learn new skills at every opportunity.

Whether you simply want a well-behaved pet, or have dreams of a working champion, your dog needs security, care, companionship, and affection. He needs rewards for good behavior, understanding of his individuality, and the chance to express natural instincts. Our job is to make sure that we learn as much as possible about our dogs, so that they are happy, healthy, and content, right into old age. Our reward? The best friend anyone could possibly have!

**Dogs are not just pets—they are members of your family.**

# You and Your Dog

**Dogs are amazing! They are loving, fun, playful, affectionate, and trusting. They can help on farms, act like eyes for the blind, protect us, work as sniffer dogs, and provide us with wonderful companionship. No other animal has built such a close relationship with people. Just like us, dogs can communicate—with one another and with us. That's why they can become our best friends!**

Of course, you will want to care for your best friend. Dogs need food, water, and a comfy place to rest. They need grooming to keep them in peak condition, exercise to keep them fit and well, and veterinary care to maintain their health. All dogs also need training to learn how to fit in with our lives, and they need companionship and security, too. Just like people, all dogs are different, and each one will have slightly different needs, depending on their age, breed, and individual likes and dislikes. Learning exactly what your dog needs can be fun—after all, the more you understand, the more you will appreciate her!

**No other animal has built such a close relationship with us.**

# Owning a dog—a companion for life

Owning a dog is both a joy and a responsibility. Your dog will be with you for the rest of his life, and it's up to you to make sure he lives every day to the fullest. Dogs give us so much—companionship, trust, loyalty, protection, and fun—that we owe it to them to make sure each stage of their life is as good as it can be.

**Puppies need to learn to settle down and be quiet with us.**

## Puppyhood

Just like a new baby, a puppy is totally dependent on his mother for his survival and growth. However, he is up on his feet very quickly and off exploring his new world. You need to take over where your puppy's mother left off. You will need to provide food, water, a place to sleep, affection, and education for your puppy, so that he fits into your life and family.

Puppies need to learn social skills to be able to communicate with other dogs and with us, and this means mixing with their own kind. Just like children going to kindergarten, puppies need to start some basic training. They should learn commands such as "sit" and "down," and to come when called. They also need to learn to have fun with other youngsters their own age. Puppy classes are an ideal way to do this, and they are great fun for us, too!

## Adolescence

At about five months of age, your puppy starts turning into an adolescent—the equivalent of a human teenager! This can sometimes be an awkward phase. Your dog may appear slightly gangly and clumsy while he grows into his legs. At this stage, it is important that you continue to give your dog lots of social contact with other dogs and people so that he can continue to develop good communication skills. Be patient and continue with his training. This stage of training is a bit like going to high school.

## Adult years

Most dogs reach their full adult size by the time they are 18 months old, but they continue to mature until they are about three years old. Some dogs develop more quickly than others. This seems to be dependent on size—very large dogs tend to develop more quickly than small ones. Once your dog is fully mature, he will continue to enjoy learning new tricks and tasks, and this will help to keep your relationship with him fun.

## Old age

Old dogs are wonderful to be with. They understand the routine of you and your family, and are completely tuned in to your feelings and actions. Although an old dog may not be quite as active as he once was in his youth, with good care, feeding, and exercise, there's no reason why he shouldn't continue to enjoy walks, training, and most of all your company, well into his advanced years!

**Dogs age faster than we do, but they are always young at heart!**

## DOG FACT

It used to be thought that one year in a human life was equivalent to seven dog years! This would make a two-year-old dog the equivalent of a 14-year-old child, and a seven-year-old dog the equivalent of a 49-year-old person. However, in recent years, more accurate calculations have been made, based on each individual dog's breed, health, and behavior. You can find these personalized tests on the Internet.

# The first days

Puppies come into the world blind, deaf, and unable to walk or run. Just like human babies, they are completely reliant on their mother for survival. However, when compared to humans, their growth rate is incredibly fast! At the point where babies are still unable to walk, dogs are full-size and can run and jump like adults!

## Chart your puppy's progress

### Birth–two weeks

Puppies are born blind and deaf. They crawl to feed from their mother and have a good sense of smell. They need their mom to keep them warm and to help them go to the toilet.

### Two weeks–four weeks

Puppies start to open their eyes at about two weeks old, but they may not be able to see very clearly. They can hear loud noises and will react to them by being startled. Puppies at this stage are the equivalent of an 18-month-old child. They can walk, but may not be very steady yet!

**Look at this puppy's face—she's "seeing" the world with her nose!**

## Four weeks–eight weeks

In four short weeks, puppies go from being entirely dependent on their mothers to being independent, inquisitive, and mischievous! They can eat solid food, walk, run, climb, and play, and love romping with their littermates! Puppies at this stage are like five-year-old children. They begin to use signals with each other, to ask other puppies to play or to show when they are annoyed. Perhaps this is a bit like playing with other children in the playground!

## Coming home

Most puppies will come to their new home when they are between 8 and 12 weeks old. It is important to remember that they have been used to having the company and comfort of their mom and littermates since the day they were born, and that they may feel a little lonely and scared when they find themselves alone for the first time. Some puppies cry at night because of this. To help her settle in, you can use a hot water bottle in your puppy's bed to give her warmth and a cuddly toy made for dogs to keep her company. You may find that your puppy sleeps better if she is near you and your family for the first few nights—after all, you have taken the place of her brothers and sisters!

*Puppies need the security of their mother until they are at least eight weeks old.*

## Busy life!

In the first few weeks in her new home, you will find that your puppy likes to eat, play, and…sleep! Sleeping is very important at this stage, so make sure your dog has a place to nap without being disturbed. A cozy basket or an indoor crate is perfect for this. Make sure that you also have lots of dog toys for your puppy to play with. Bear in mind that she will want to chew, and that to begin with, she won't be able to tell the difference between her chew toys and your favorite playthings! Keep your toys out of the way so your puppy learns that they are yours and should not be touched.

# House rules

Having a puppy is exciting and fun, but it's important that your puppy settles into a good routine to help him feel happy and secure. Make sure your family decides together on the house rules you are going to set for your puppy—and that all of you follow them.

### Sleep well

Decide on where your puppy is going to sleep—and stick to it. If you let your puppy sleep under the blanket when he's small and cute, he'll still expect to do the same when he's huge and muddy! Make sure your pup has a cozy bed somewhere quiet, and allow him to sleep undisturbed.

An indoor kennel may look like a cage to us, but can offer security and safety.

### Sitting pretty

Allowing your dog on the furniture is a personal choice. Think about how large he is going to be and how hairy! If you decide it's best that he doesn't climb on the sofa or the chairs, then start as you intend to go on.

### Dinnertime

Your dog needs his own food bowl and water dish, and needs peace and quiet while he is eating. To make sure your pup isn't worried that you'll take his food away from him, it is a good idea to sometimes drop delicious extra bits of food into his bowl while he's eating. That way, he will trust that you give food, not take it away.

What a good puppy. Learning to wait in your basket is difficult!

**TOP TIP**

Most puppies aren't very happy about being picked up, and there's a good reason for this. In the wild, only very tiny puppies are picked up by their parents and their canine carers. After the age of about six weeks, a dog would only be picked up if he were under attack! For this reason, it's important that you only ever pick up your puppy with an adult to help you. Make sure you place one hand under the puppy's bottom to support his body weight and hold him securely, as he may get hurt if he falls.

**Be careful with me!
Remember to hold
your pup securely.**

## Table manners

Be strict with your whole family: Never feed your dog from the table or from your plates when you are eating. If you give your dog tidbits of your food, even occasionally, don't be surprised when he sits next to you drooling, or tries to mug you for your snacks! Ask your dog to go to his bed when you are eating your breakfast, lunch, or dinner, or even if you are eating a snack. Give him a chew toy to enjoy there so that he's happy—and distracted.

## Your dog's dictionary

Dogs need to learn the meaning of every word we use with them. It is no good assuming that your puppy will understand his name, the word "no," or even "good dog" until he has made associations with them. In order to help your dog understand what you want, it's helpful to make a dictionary for him, so that everyone in the family uses the same words. For example, if you want to ask your dog to lie down, decide whether you want him to respond to "down," "flat," or "lie down." When you have decided which commands you are going to use, write each one in a dictionary like the one below and stick it on the fridge door for everyone to see!

| Word | Action |
| --- | --- |
| e.g., "Down" | "Shadow to lie down immediately" |
|  |  |
|  |  |
|  |  |

# Hazards in the home and outdoors

Puppies come equipped with a full set of teeth that a shark would be proud of!
They love to chew and chomp on things because this helps soothe their teething
irritations. It's fun, too! For these reasons, most puppies chew a lot. It's up to us to
protect them from chewing dangerous items or from swallowing things that may do
them harm.

## In your home

There are lots of things in your home that may harm your dog if she gets hold of them or eats them. Some of them may seem quite innocent to us, but are dangerous to your dog. For example, people love chocolate, but it is poisonous to dogs. Raisins and onions can cause them problems, too.

Toys are fun to play with, but make sure your dog can't chew them up or swallow them. Balls that are too small can get wedged in your dog's throat very easily. Dogs sometimes try to chew other items, too. Cassette tape is highly dangerous, as it can become wrapped around your dog's intestines. Objects like needles and elastic bands also pose a serious threat.

Be very careful to keep human medicines and household chemicals, such as cleaning fluids, out of reach of your curious puppy. Even one or two tablets can make your dog seriously ill.

**Keep chemicals out of your dog's reach.**

## In the yard

Your puppy probably loves playing in the yard or garden, but here too you need to make sure she's safe. Some plants can be toxic to dogs, and eating flower bulbs is highly dangerous.

Make sure you keep your dog away from machinery, such as the lawn mower, and never allow her to go near chemicals such as antifreeze, which is highly poisonous.

**Curious dogs will sniff around everywhere. You need to make sure they don't find anything that will hurt them.**

## Out and about

We love taking our dogs out, but you need to be your dog's guardian angel outdoors, too. Keep her close to you and on the leash if you are near traffic, if there are other animals nearby, or if you do not know the area. There are laws about dogs in some areas, so look for signs and don't let your dog off the leash if there is no adult with you to supervise. No matter how tempting it might be, do not throw sticks for her to chase. They can easily break apart into sharp splinters and get stuck in her mouth or throat, which can be very dangerous.

## Think like a dog!

The best way to keep your dog safe is to train her to walk nicely on the leash and to come back when you call her. It also helps to think like her! To most dogs, gaps in fences look inviting, pieces of your food and small objects can be tempting to eat and animals are fun to chase. Instinctive types of behavior can put your dog at risk—it's up to us to make sure that they are safe.

## QUICK QUIZ

Do you know how to keep your puppy safe? Circle an answer for each question, then add up your score at the end to see how safe your puppy is!

**1. Which of these human foods is poisonous to your puppy?**
a) Oranges
b) Chocolate
c) Milk

**2. What should you do if your puppy looks sick?**
a) Take her to the vet
b) Give her a pat
c) Cover her up with a blanket

**3. Your puppy has picked up a sharp stick and wants you to play with her. You should:**
a) Throw the stick for her to fetch
b) Distract her so she drops the stick and forgets all about it
c) Chase her so you can take the stick away

**4. Your puppy is bored while you watch TV. She tries chewing the table leg. You should:**
a) Tell her off for being naughty
b) Ignore her. You don't want to miss your favorite program
c) Get her a chew toy to keep her occupied

**5. You take your puppy for a walk to a place you don't know. Do you:**
a) Let her off the leash so she can explore right away?
b) Keep her on the leash until you know if there are any roads or other animals close by, or if there are any laws about dogs in that area.

Answers: 1. (b) 2. (a) 3. (b) 4. (c) 5. (b)

# Health and grooming

Grooming should be done every day. It keeps your dog healthy and clean, and allows you to check for illnesses and fleas. It also builds your bond with him. Keep grooming fun and enjoyable and your dog will happily be brushed every day!

**Teach your dog to sit still to be brushed and combed. The brush is not a toy!**

## Brushing

The equipment you need depends on what type of coat your dog has, but it should never be sharp or uncomfortable. If your dog has a smooth, short coat like a boxer's or pug's:

**1** First use a rubber brush to loosen dead skin, dirt, and loose hair.

**2** Put a shine on your dog's coat by stroking with a chamois cloth or a velvet mitt.

Many popular breeds, like the golden retriever and German shepherd, have a double coat. A soft undercoat serves as a protective barrier against the cold. The harsher top coat is water-resistant.

**1** Use a slick brush to remove dead hair and debris from the inner and outer coat.

**2** Now work on the undercoat with a wide-tooth comb.

**3** Be very gentle when you comb areas that are prone to matting, such as behind the ears, mane, and legs.

Once you have given your dog a good brushing, it's time to check his ears, eyes, and teeth.

### TOP TIP

Some owners like to brush their dog's teeth with a special toothbrush and doggy toothpaste. You will need to gradually get your dog used to this, as it's a strange sensation for the dog at first. However, the temptation of liver-flavored toothpaste always helps!

## Checking ears

With a food treat in one hand, carefully lift each of your dog's ear flaps so you can look inside. They should look pink and clean, and have no smell or brown discharge. If there is a discharge, or if your dog has been scratching at his ears or holding his head to one side, it may mean that he has an ear infection. This will need treatment from the vet. Never push anything into the ear, but wipe the flap with damp cotton balls if you need to. Give your dog the food treat for being patient!

## Checking eyes

Your dog's eyes should look clean and bright, with no redness or discharge. Dogs have a third eyelid, which covers the eye when the dog is unwell. This can be an indicator that he needs to go to the vet.

## Checking teeth

With a food treat in one hand, use the other to gently lift his lips on one side, then the other, so that you can see his teeth. Do they look clean and white? A bad odor or lots of yellow staining might mean that your dog needs to have his teeth checked by a vet. Give your dog the treat for being good during his checkup!

### GROOMING GAME

Line up 10 treats in a row on a table or windowsill where your dog can see them but cannot reach them. Brush or handle one part of your dog's body from the list below, then give him one treat as a reward for being still. Continue through the list until you have groomed all 10 parts and he has had all his treats!

1. Brush his tail.
2. Pick up his left front paw and examine his nails.
3. Brush his back legs.
4. Look at his teeth.
5. Examine his ear.
6. Brush from head to tail along his back.
7. Look in his eyes.
8. Brush his chest.
9. Examine his back right foot.
10. Brush his tummy.

**Grooming your dog will help build a bond of trust between you. Try to groom him every day.**

### DOG FACT

Your dog cannot tell you if he's not feeling well. The only way he can let you know is by behaving strangely. Watch out for signs your dog may not be well. He may be quiet, lack energy, want to sleep or drink more, or he may be irritable. Always take your dog to be checked by a vet if you are worried about his health or behavior.

# Exercise

One of the best aspects of owning a dog is being able to take her for walks and have fun outdoors! Exercise is good for our pets, and for us, but going on the same walk every day gets a little dull. Instead, try to think up new adventures and activities that involve the whole family. Remember to look out for any hazards to your dog!

### TOP TIP
Think about what makes your dog happy (*see page 40 for inspiration*). If you own a terrier, chances are she will like chasing and digging! If you own a sporting dog, she may well like swimming and retrieving. Check out some of these other ideas as well.

**Swimming is great exercise. Some dog breeds even have webbed feet to help them move through the water!**

## Hide-and-seek adventure

If you are lucky enough to be able to take your dog to the local park, make the most of the space there. Spread out and play hide-and-seek. Hold your dog until one of you has hidden behind a tree, then send her to find them! Once she finds them, this person then holds her collar and the game starts all over again!

## In the swim

Many dogs love to swim. Some breeds, such as Newfoundlands, were bred to do this. The huge Newfoundland has a special coat and even webbed feet to help drive her through the water. Doggy swimming pools are available in many areas. Other perfect places for a dip include lakes, streams, and, of course, the sea. However, do make sure that the edge of the water has a shallow area where your dog can climb out easily. If your dog has not been swimming before, start gently and allow her to go in at her own pace. Build her confidence gradually. Never push your dog into the water—it may put her off for life!

## Activity park

Going to the woods? Enjoy the obstacles that nature gives you! Encourage your dog to climb up on tree stumps and walk along fallen trunks. She can leap over branches and scramble through bushes, just like she's on an obstacle course. Use a food treat to encourage your dog to begin.

## Soccer crazy

Many dogs are ace soccer players! Some are best at moving the ball, while others make great goalies. Find out what your dog is good at. If your dog has not played before, start by teaching her to nudge the ball with her head or nose. Most dogs will do this if you dribble the ball rather than kicking it hard. Praise your dog and nudge it back to her if she pushes it your way. Some dogs like to try to grab the ball with their teeth! If yours does this, you may need to start her soccer training with a hard ball that she can't burst!

**All dogs love to go out. Good training will mean you're proud to take her anywhere.**

### DOG FACT

Dogs will need different amounts of exercise, depending on their breed, age, and fitness level. Puppies should have no more than two 20-minute walks per day, as their joints and bones have not yet properly formed. After the age of one year, most breeds (except giant breeds like Great Danes and Saint Bernards) can cope with as much exercise as you can give them, but build it up gradually to avoid injury.

# Learning Dog Language

**Dogs don't speak English! Dogs communicate using their body language and facial expressions. They also make a range of sounds, such as woofs, yips, growls, and whines. Unlike us, they have the extra advantage of being able to communicate through their heightened sense of smell. Dogs can recognize each other and us by scent alone!**

Learning to understand your dog's body language will allow you to "read" how your dog is feeling: whether he's happy, excited, angry, or confused. This means you will be able to respond accordingly. Just like us, dogs have different feelings, but these are often misunderstood by people who haven't taken the time to learn dog language. Learning any new language takes time and patience. You may need to practice looking at your dog and asking yourself what he is thinking and feeling. However, all this homework is worth it. You'll be able to communicate with your dog and to make sure that you and your best friend understand each other.

**Take the time to learn dog language. You'll be glad you did!**

# Learning "canine" as a second language

**Learning "canine" as a new language can be fun and exciting! If you are good at watching your dog and noticing all the tiny signals that she gives, you will become an expert in no time.**

**Dogs watch us all the time and learn our body language. We need to do the same!**

### Super senses

Some dog signals are easy to understand, because they're similar to those that humans use. However, others are very different. We can't assume that dogs always understand us!

Have you ever noticed that dogs watch everything that's going on? Some dogs can even learn to predict when we're going out, or when visitors are about to arrive! This is not a sixth sense but the ability to detect even tiny changes in our behavior. These changes tell the dog that something is about to happen.

Dogs are so good at this that some are even trained to detect when a person is going to have an epileptic seizure. These dogs can predict seizures up to an hour before they happen, which gives the people time to get to safety and to get medical help.

## TOP TIP
Try to imagine what it must be like to be a dog for a day, living in the world of humans! Imagine meeting lots of people who all behave, look, sound, and smell very different. We all talk and make lots of noise, and then expect our dogs to pick up on commands that we give them. It must be very confusing!

## DOG FACT
Although different breeds of dog look very different, all dogs speak the same language and understand one another. However, they need to practice their social skills by playing with each other and with us when they are puppies.

## It's rude to stare

Dogs use eye contact to communicate with one another, and with us. Direct staring is a little threatening to dogs, as it is for humans. We also feel uncomfortable if someone stares at us. For this reason, some dogs don't like to look directly at their owners—they are being polite by looking away!

**Dogs come in all shapes and sizes, but need to learn to read each other no matter what they look like!**

## Humans are weird

Just as we have to learn the meaning of our dogs' postures and signals, so dogs have to learn what humans mean by their words and gestures. Think about what you look and sound like from your dog's point of view. When you smile, you show your teeth, but you are being friendly! In dog language, this could be trouble. When you play, you run, scream, and shout. It's all good fun to us, but dogs have to learn that you are not hurt or behaving like prey! Human beings behave in ways that must seem very odd to dogs. If this weren't enough, we must also look and smell very odd to our dogs. We wear glasses and hats, men sometimes have beards and women put on makeup and perfumes. These things must make us look and smell very different to our pets. Perhaps it's no wonder that dogs sometimes get scared of people who look different. Imagine what it must be like for a dog meeting someone wearing a motorcycle helmet for the first time!

**What do you think these two collies are "saying" with their body language?**

# Dog language: Tails and bodies

Dogs' tails are an important part of their communication systems. It's tempting to think that dogs are always happy when they wag their tails, but it's much more complex and subtle. They can signal happiness, anger, uncertainty, and fear—all through the height and movement of their tails.

### Big open wags
Dogs express friendliness and greetings through their tails. This is most commonly shown in big, mid-height, open tail wags. Where the dog's tail is doing this, and his facial expression is relaxed and friendly, you can be sure he's pleased to see you!

### Windmill greetings!
Some dogs are so thrilled to see you that their tails go round and round, like a windmill! This is caused by the tail wag being so big that it has to go round, not just from side to side. Perhaps this is the equivalent of a huge grin!

### Tail tucked under
If you see a dog with its tail tucked right underneath its body, chances are that it is not at all happy, and is probably scared of something or someone. The dog clamps its tail underneath to protect its belly and underside.

### Tail wagging low
Dogs often wag their tails when they are uncertain about a situation, but typically they will wag very low. Sometimes their tails seem clamped to their back legs. It's thought that the movement of the tail helps to spread their scent, so the low wag would tell other dogs that they were worried.

### Stiff, upright tail
Dogs that are feeling tense or angry may hold their tails still or upright. Sometimes their tails might even appear to vibrate when they wag. This is like a red flag to other dogs, signaling danger!

## DOG FACT

It is thought that dogs' tails act as visual signals to other dogs, to show them how they are feeling and to indicate their intentions. It's likely that tail movements also help to spread the dog's scent, which gives information, too.

This little dog is being friendly, but looks unsure. How does his body say this?

## Body talk

A dog's legs and body posture will also give you clues as to how he is feeling. Frightened dogs will crouch, to keep their bodies low to the ground. Bold or aggressive dogs will walk with stiff legs, to make themselves look as large as possible.

Dogs that are relaxed and friendly tend to move their bodies in a flowing, flexible way. They may sway or writhe in a snakelike fashion to get close to you, especially when saying hello. Some dogs get so excited when greeting people that they wag their whole rear ends, not just their tails!

Something has caught this Labrador's attention!

## DOG FACT

Both dogs and people give away clues about how they are feeling in their body language and facial expression. You only have to watch a movie to see this in action. Imagine someone who is acting frightened. Perhaps they are creeping along. Their movements are short and sharp, and they keep their body as small as possible to avoid being seen. Very often, they will keep quite still, and only their eyes move as they watch for danger. Dogs behave like this when they are frightened, too!

# Dog language: Face and head

**Dogs show a lot of emotion through their facial expressions and the way they move their heads and ears. Take a close look at her eyes, ears, and mouth to understand what she's saying.**

### The eyes have it

In dog language, direct staring is nearly always interpreted as a threat. This is common for many species of animal, including humans, but is especially true for dogs, who need to learn early that it's much safer to avert their gaze than to look a new dog in the eye directly. Their mother will have started to teach them this in the litter, by staring hard at them if they were behaving in an inappropriate way and then following up on this stare with a snap or growl if necessary.

### All ears!

Ear positions are important to dogs. Unfortunately, the messages that ears give are often confused, as we have bred dogs that now have long, heavy ears that cannot move so well. However, in breeds that have highly mobile, upright ears, ear messages can clearly be seen. For example, ears pointed upright and forward show that the dog is alert and ready for action. Ears that are held back, or are pinned to the head, show that the dog is feeling anxiety or fear. Of course, humans cannot move their ears to show how they are feeling!

**These ears are upright and alert, but the expression is soft and non-threatening.**

**A stare can be threatening, but this dog seems friendly.**

## Head start

Dogs have a variety of different head shapes, depending on their breed. Some, such as the dachshund, are long and pointy. Others are broad and have short muzzles, such as the boxer or the pug. The shape of a dog's head will determine whether her skin is smooth or wrinkly, which can make a difference to the messages that the dog is giving. Dogs that are alert and friendly tend to keep their heads upright, with the skin on the top smooth. Dogs that are showing aggression may push their heads forward and wrinkle their foreheads, almost like a human frown.

## Big mouth!

Dogs have very large mouths, long tongues, and big teeth. This is because they are designed to be hunters and to kill prey, then rip it apart to eat it. The long fangs at the front of a dog's mouth are called the canine teeth, and are designed for stabbing and tearing. The teeth at the back of the mouth

### DOG FACT

Dogs might use their tongues to show how they are feeling. If your dog licks her lips, or flicks her tongue over her nose, she might be feeling anxious or stressed.

are called molars. These are good for chewing and crushing bones. A dog's set of teeth is an amazing weapon. Dogs can react and bite very quickly, and can do a great deal of damage. For this reason, they have developed good communication skills to make sure they settle disputes between themselves without resorting to violence. This could result in serious injury! Dogs are a sociable and peaceable species and like to avoid conflict. They are very good at controlling their mouths and covering their teeth to show that they're friendly. This is the opposite of humans, who show their teeth when they smile!

**Dogs use their mouths to eat, drink, pant, yawn, play, and show affection and aggression.**

## DOG TEETH

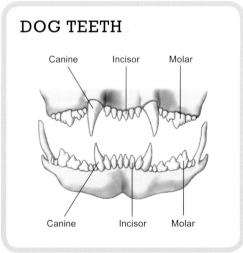

Canine    Incisor    Molar

Canine    Incisor    Molar

# Dog language: Scent

A dog's sense of smell far outstrips that of a human. They have 25 times more scent receptors in their noses. It is said that they can detect one drop of blood in five quarts of water! We all know that dogs can find things, and even people, by using their noses, but did you know that they also gather important information about you, other dogs, and the world around them, just by sniffing?

## Scent signals

There's little doubt that to a dog, sniffing the grass where other dogs have been is a bit like reading a newspaper. Information on who's been there, how long ago, and even how healthy they were may all be left as scent signals for other dogs to examine.

As soon as they're born, puppies have a good sense of smell. Well before they can see or hear properly, a puppy can detect and distinguish between different smells. When you look at a newborn puppy, you will see that it is practically all nose!

**Who came this way? How long ago? Do I know them? All this information and more is probably contained in scent signals.**

Puppies learn to recognize smells very quickly. This helps to keep them safe as they can identify their own mother and siblings.

As a dog grows, he learns that all dogs and humans smell different, and that other information—about their gender, health, and perhaps even their emotional state—can be gleaned from sniffing them.

## DOG FACT

Have you noticed that some dogs try to leave their smell as high up and obvious as possible? Male dogs may cock their legs to get their urine as high as possible up vertical objects, and some dogs try to deposit their feces on top of tree stumps or a mound of earth. This is so they can leave long-distance signals that can easily be read by other dogs once they're gone. Dogs that scratch the earth up around where they have been are also trying to draw attention to their "messages."

**Sniffing is the doggy equivalent of shaking hands! Dogs introduce themselves by using scent.**

Because most of the scent-producing glands in a dog's body are clustered around the base of the tail, dogs tend to sniff that area to gain the most information. Thankfully, they quickly learn to sniff our hands instead!

## Clan odor

Although humans have a poor sense of smell in comparison to dogs, it's interesting that we do respond to the scent of our own individual family, and that we can recognize the smell of our loved ones very easily. It's thought that we start to smell alike if we live with one another. In just the same way, it's likely that dogs that live in a social group also start to smell alike—that this helps them to recognize one another and to keep the bonds in the group strong. No one knows if humans and dogs living in the same family all start to smell similar. It might happen!

## SMELL TEST

When out in the woods, pick up and hold a piece of stick in your bare hands for a period of about 30 seconds. Now place that stick back on the ground without your dog seeing —being careful not to touch any other sticks around it. Now call your dog and see if he can find the stick that you touched! Dogs that are used to this game will search for the right one and will not settle for any other even though they all look the same. Remember: Don't let your dog pick up and chew on the stick, as it may be sharp. Train him to just identify it, perhaps by touching it with his paw.

# Dog language: Vocalizations

Dogs don't use words, but they do use a full range of barks, yips, whines, growls, and woofs! Puppies learn these sounds for long-distance communication, as well as to get a message across to more than one member of the family at a time.

**Woof! There are various types of barking. Each type says something different.**

## Whines and cries

Pups rely totally on their mother for food, warmth, and protection. However, they have a good set of lungs and can give a high-pitched distress cry if they find themselves alone and hungry. This cry has a powerful influence over the mother, who can't ignore it. In one experiment, a tape recording of a puppy crying was played to a new mother, and she left her other puppies to go bring the tape recorder into the nest! Into adulthood, dogs will whimper to express pain, fear, or cold, but will give a high-pitched whine when very excited, such as when going out for a walk!

**This dog is barking encouragement to her friend! She lifts one paw in a playful gesture.**

## Yips

Even big dogs can make small yipping noises. These are often designed to show that they are feeling playful, or to get attention. They tend to be produced by making a noise in the mouth, while keeping the lips closed as much as possible. This keeps the teeth covered, and therefore ensures that the gesture is non-threatening.

## Barks

One major difference between wolves and dogs is that wolves never bark! Domestic dogs bark for lots of different reasons—because they are bored or excited, to locate other dogs and people, and to warn of intruders. The tone and pitch of a dog's bark varies, depending on what she is trying to say. One very deep "oooof" is usually a warning bark that strangers are around, while a volley of short, sharp barks means "keep away."

## Howls

Wolves are the masters of howling. We all know that familiar sound, and how they look when they throw their heads back and howl at the moon! Domestic dogs also howl from time to time, and some breeds—such as huskies, malamutes, and Eskimo dogs—are more likely to howl than others. Dogs tend to howl to try to make contact with members of their family if they are lonely, or to call their family together when out on a "hunt." Some dogs will also howl when triggered by a piece of music or singing. Perhaps it sounds like howling to them!

### DOG FACT

Growling during play may sound the same as aggressive growling, but the dog looks very different. She will be enjoying the game and will show soft body language, squinty eyes, and lots of play signals.

## Growls

Dogs growl when they're upset or angry, but also when they're playing. This can be confusing, so it's important to look at the rest of the dog's body language and facial expression to know what she means. Growls are like an early warning system. If the dog is very still, if she shows the whites around her eyes, or if she stares, then the growl is a threat. If unheeded, the dog may decide to bite to make the person or other dog go away.

**Howling is a very powerful sound and harks back to the dog's ancestry.**

**Growling is a warning—aggression comes next!**

# When it's time to play!

You can learn to "talk" to your dog and understand what he is "saying" by watching his body language and his face. For example, instead of smiling to show that they are happy, dogs wag their tails and use relaxed facial expressions to show that they are content.

### Play bow

The clearest of all play signals! The dog puts his head low to the ground and his bottom and tail high in the air, as if he is going to pounce. This is an invitation to play, even though it may look a little as if the dog is stalking prey!

### Paw raises

Dogs that are feeling playful will often bat at you or another dog with a paw, by raising it up at the elbow and patting it down. This is a bit like us shaking hands and shows that the dog is friendly and feeling playful.

### Bounces

Some dogs, especially puppies, will bounce so that their two front feet pounce on the ground in front of us or another dog. Pups will sometimes bounce, then run away, as an invitation to be chased.

### Play face

Dogs often put on a play face when they are enjoying a game: Their ears are forward, their foreheads wrinkled, and their lips drawn back into a "smiley" grin. They may also bark to get attention, but this will sound high-pitched and yappy rather than deep and booming.

**Playtime! This is a classic play bow with the bottom and tail in the air. The head is low with eye contact.**

**This little dog clearly wants to play. She raises her paw and nudges at the ball as a hint!**

## Hip swings

Some dogs, especially big, bouncy ones like German shepherds and Labradors, will play by knocking their "opponent" out of the way by spinning around and nudging them with their hip.

## Wrestling matches

Dogs that are evenly matched in terms of confidence will often "wrestle" with each other by biting each other's legs, ears, and faces. One may even flop onto its back and let the other one stand over him while they play bite. Once they've had a good wrestle like this, it's common for them to swap places, so that the other one is then on top!

## Toy temptations

Dogs that want to play will often bring you a toy or even an object they have stolen! They typically show you what they have, then dash off at high speed in an attempt to get you to chase them. Sometimes, they may turn around with the toy in their mouth and try a play bow, to tempt you to come closer.

### DOG FACT

Although dogs love to play by wrestling and biting each other, they do so by following strict rules that keep them safe. Because of this, you are better off playing with your dog using a toy they can chase and tug. Never allow your dog to bite at your mouth, skin, clothes, or hair. These games are not safe and should always be avoided.

**These young dogs are taking turns being the boss in a play fight.**

# If your dog is feeling scared

Just like us, dogs sometimes get frightened. They may be scared of loud noises, other dogs, or new experiences. Dogs show that they are anxious by using body signals, by trying to hide, and by preparing to run away. If you can spot these signs early, you can help your dog to feel more confident—a bit like being her big brother or sister!

**"I'm worried."** This dog's tail is tucked under and his rear end is sloping downward.

## Pretend I'm not here!

Some dogs simply try to pretend that they can't be seen when they are scared. They may go completely still in order to blend into the background. This is called "freezing." Other dogs may turn their heads away, or may sniff the ground, so as not to be noticed.

## Disappearing act

Dogs often try to shrink when they feel threatened! They do this by cowering, so that their body lowers to the ground and their tail is tucked right underneath. Typically, dogs that are scared also flatten their ears to their heads. They may have wide, staring eyes, just like people do when they feel frightened.

## Look closely

Nearly all dogs lick their lips when they feel anxious. You might even see the dog's tongue flick up and over her nose—a sure sign she's worried. Dogs will also blink a lot if they feel stressed, and may yawn. This is often misinterpreted as boredom or tiredness.

## Brave support

Understanding how your dog is feeling is the first step on the way to helping her. Unless it's for fun when you're watching a scary movie, no one likes being scared, so you need to help your dog feel more confident.

## How to calm your dog

If you spot your dog showing signs of worry, think about what might be frightening her. Is it another dog? Perhaps she's scared of loud noises. Maybe she doesn't like something

## DOG FACT

One of the biggest mistakes people often make is to believe their dog is looking guilty when she has done something wrong. Dogs often look away, put their ears back, and hang their heads when their owners are angry, but this body language is showing fear, not guilt!

## TOP TIP

Resist the temptation to pat or pet your dog if she is showing signs of being scared, as it could make matters worse. Instead, try to distract her with a treat or a toy, or wait until she's feeling braver and wants to play again.

that's happening to her, or she anticipates something unpleasant—such as a trip to the vet. If you can see what is frightening your dog, try to remove her from the situation if you can, until she's calmed down.

Sometimes it's not possible to protect your dog from something scary. For example, dogs are often scared of thunder and lightning or fireworks. In these cases, it's very important that you don't accidentally reward her for being scared! Of course you will want to reassure her, but because dogs don't understand English, this can seem like praise for cowardly behavior. To avoid this, it is best to give your dog a safe area to go, such as behind the sofa or under a blanket, and then ignore her completely. Only praise her and give her attention when she recovers and is being brave once again!

**Pet your dog when she has recovered and is being brave again. Don't reward scaredy-dogs!**

# Anger—what are the signs?

**Like humans, dogs can become angry if they feel threatened. Most dogs would rather run away when they're scared, but if their options are limited—by being held on the leash, for example—then they might strike out. Some dogs will also be aggressive to keep food or toys all for themselves!**

**Never approach a dog that is tied up. Some dogs might react badly if they can't escape.**

Dogs have a wide range of signals they use to warn others if they are feeling angry or defensive. These signals are designed to give others a chance to keep out of their way, so that more serious conflict—fights and bites—don't happen. Dogs are a peace-loving species and will generally choose to avoid conflict whenever they can. Learning their warning signals is very important!

## Freezing

This warning signal can be very quick, or can last several seconds or even minutes. The dog's body and head will go completely still. The dog even seems to hold his breath!

## Stiff body

A dog with a stiff body and tail is showing tension in his muscles as he prepares for flight (running away) or fight (aggression). Sometimes the dog's legs will move in a stiff, almost wooden fashion, with slow, deliberate movements.

**Always be careful around a dog that has a bone or other possession.**

## TOP TIP

No matter how well you think you understand dogs, you must always ask permission before you pet a dog that belongs to someone else. Never touch a dog when you are out on your own.

## Staring

No one likes being stared at! Direct, staring eye contact is a threat in dog language, just as it can be in humans. Sometimes the dog's eyes will look black. Fear or anxiety causes the dark center of the eye, the pupil, to dilate or widen. This happens to us when we're scared, too.

## Growling

Growling is a dog's way of saying, "Don't come any closer." Although dogs sometimes growl when they are play fighting, a dog that is growling over an item or food, or while it is being touched or looked at, is clearly giving a warning that it may bite.

## Snarling

A dog's snarl is a bit like us shouting at someone. It's a clear warning: The dog uses sound, in a type of throaty growl, and a visual signal, by showing his teeth. This demonstrates what impressive weapons he has. He doesn't really want to use them, but he will if he has to.

## Lunging and snapping

Dogs can move with lightning speed. They also have great control over their reactions and bodies. This means that a dog may lunge forward, as if to bite, but may bark or snap instead, without making contact. This response is designed to make another dog or a person jump backward, stand still, or run away. It's often a final warning, which should be heeded!

## Traffic light safety system!

**Green light – approach with permission.**
You know the dog well and he greets you like an old friend. He has a soft face, a relaxed body, and squinty eyes. His tail gives big, wide wags, or goes round and round like a windmill.

**Amber – be cautious. Don't touch!**
You don't know the dog very well. He does not approach you and seems worried. He licks his lips and his body looks a bit tense. His tail may be held low and wagging. He may pretend you're not there.

**Red light – move away slowly. Don't touch!**
You may or may not know the dog, but he is stiff and tense and is staring at you. He may growl or bark and may show his teeth, or may simply stand still, watching you all the time.

**If a dog is snarling like this, he is giving a clear warning!**

# How your dog says, "I'm happy!"

A happy dog is usually easy to spot. Bright eyes, a wagging tail, and a friendly, open expression will let you know!

**A happy face and a happy tail means a happy dog!**

## Welcome home

Dogs are always pleased to see us when we get home, and sometimes even when we have only been in another room for a few minutes! Dogs greet family members by asking for attention and enjoying our contact. Many dogs will use their whole bodies to express their happiness, and become wiggly and squirmy in their movements. Some dogs will wag their tail so hard that it goes round and round, or they will wag it very hard from side to side.

Some dogs might jump up to greet people. While this may not be very polite, it is a friendly gesture. The dog is trying to get as close to your face as possible! Other dogs may go get a toy to bring to the person they are greeting, like a kind of gift.

## Love me

Most dogs love affection and like to be stroked and touched, particularly on the chest and rump. Many dogs ask for this attention by approaching the person and resting their head against them, looking up with soft, squinty eyes. Who can resist?

Your dog might also give you a paw to get attention. This gesture comes from the time when she was a newborn puppy. Back then, she would press her mother's belly with her paws to ask for milk: Feelings of relief and comfort became associated with this action.

**These puppies are blissfully content.**

## DOG FACT

Did you know that it's bad manners to try to stroke a dog on the head? Reaching for a dog's head can be a little threatening, and most dogs much prefer to be touched on the chest or tummy.

## HAPPINESS CHECKLIST

Do you know what makes your dog happy? Check the boxes that you think apply.

- ☐ Stroking on the chest
- ☐ Playing with toys
- ☐ Food!
- ☐ Playing hide-and-seek
- ☐ Being scratched on the rump
- ☐ Chase games
- ☐ Being calm and sleepy with you

Dogs can also ask for affection in more subtle ways. Some may approach and then turn around to offer their rump for a scratch. This might seem odd to us, but it's the dog's way of saying, "I'm no threat. I have no teeth at that end. Please pet me!"

Dogs learn very quickly how to get attention from humans. Some figure out that gentle, quiet behaviors are ignored, while barking, standing right in front of the television, and throwing toys around are guaranteed ways to get noticed!

## Sleepy contentment

Dogs are often at their happiest when they are calm and content. Sleepy dogs may sigh deeply, wag their tails softly when you talk to them, and make contented sounds as they fall asleep. Watch to see if your dog wants to be touching you as she slumbers. Many dogs love being with their owners so much that they will snooze peacefully while they can feel their owner next to them, but will wake up and follow them if they get up!

**Many dogs love being scratched around the base of the tail and will keep asking for more!**

# Understanding different dog breeds

There are literally hundreds of different breeds of dog in the world. Not only do they vary in looks but they all behave differently, too. This is because they have been bred to do certain jobs—such as herding or guarding. If you own a mixed breed or mutt, learn the kinds of tasks your dog enjoys by experimenting!

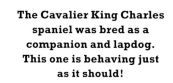

**The Cavalier King Charles spaniel was bred as a companion and lapdog. This one is behaving just as it should!**

## Hounds

Hounds were chosen for their ability to spot prey and track it down by scent or sight. Some breeds, such as foxhounds and beagles, were bred to hunt in packs. These dogs have developed an unusual way of communicating with one another when hunting—they make a sound that is a mixture of a bark and a howl, called baying. Sight hounds, or gaze hounds, as they are sometimes called, have excellent eyesight and can spot a moving target in the distance. This group includes the beautiful Afghan hound and the greyhound.

**Hounds were bred for tracking prey by sight or scent.**

## DOG FACT

Cocker spaniels have very long ears. When they can find nothing else to carry, some have been known to carry their own floppy ears in their mouths!

# Herding and "pastoral" breeds

These are the dogs you will see rounding up sheep, cattle, and even geese. They tend to be very quick and are responsive to their owners. Because of this, herding breeds such as border collies are excellent at doggy sports, like flyball and agility. However, they love to chase and herd so much that they may get into trouble for trying to round up people!

# Sporting dogs

Finding and retrieving during hunting trips— that's what these dogs were bred for. Many popular breeds, such as golden retrievers, Labradors, and cocker spaniels, are in this group. These breeds still behave in ways that show they enjoy this kind of work. Many love to retrieve and often like picking up an article to bring to you in greeting. Most of these dogs also adore water—and wading in muddy puddles!

## DOG FACT
Some breeds may not look like herding dogs, but their ancestors were used to round up cattle and they still have the same instincts. Lancashire heelers and corgis may have short legs, but they have amazing stamina and were bred to nip at the heels of sheep and cows to make them move forward!

# Working and utility breeds

This group of dogs were bred to help humans in their work. Some, like the Bernese mountain dog, pulled carts, while others, like the Doberman, acted as guards. The Dalmatian was bred to run behind horse-drawn carriages, in the days before we had cars. They would protect the rich lords and ladies from highwaymen when they were traveling.

# Toy dogs

Not real toys, of course—but often tiny—toy dogs are sometimes referred to as lapdogs, because they can snuggle on your lap for a cuddle! Many toy dogs still have the instincts of their bigger cousins and shouldn't be treated any differently. They love to run, jump, and play, and can take part in training and dog sports like any other breed. Yorkshire terriers and Cavalier King Charles spaniels are particularly good fun, and will always be happy to join in with your activities.

**Terriers still possess strong instincts to dig, since this is what they were bred to do.**

# Canine quiz

Check out the pictures and see if you can tell what the dog is "saying." Choose option a, b, or c for each picture, then add up your score to see how well you can "speak dog"!

## 1

- **a** I'm frightened.
- **b** I'm happy to be with you.
- **c** I'm playful.

## 2

- **a** I'm asking you to chase me.
- **b** I'm aggressive and dangerous.
- **c** I'm calm and alert.

## 3

- **a** I'm bored.
- **b** I'm angry— keep away.
- **c** I'm friendly— please pet me.

## 4

- **a** I'm frightened and want to run away.
- **b** I'm asking you to play.
- **c** I want you to go away.

# 5

- **a** This is mine—keep away.
- **b** I'm happy to share this with you.
- **c** I'm just looking after this for a friend!

# 6

- **a** Hello, nice to meet you!
- **b** I don't like you —go away!
- **c** I'm just thinking about my lunch.

# 7

- **a** I love you!
- **b** I'm going to bite you!
- **c** I'm not sure about you yet.

# 8

- **a** Hello! Please train me!
- **b** I'm sad, leave me alone.
- **c** I'm not interested in you.

# 9

- **a** I'm happy to see you!
- **b** I don't know you —keep away!
- **c** Please play with me!

# 10

- **a** I'm feeling guilty – I know I've done wrong.
- **b** I'm happy and cheerful.
- **c** You seem a bit angry, and it makes me worried.

**Your score:**
1–3 correct: More practice required. Have another try!
4–6 correct: Good. Keep watching those dogs!
7–9 correct: Very good. You can speak "canine" well.
10 out of 10: Excellent! You are a dog language expert!

**Answers:**
1. a, 2. c, 3. b, 4. b, 5. a, 6. a, 7. c, 8. c, 9. b, 10. c

# How to Speak Dog

Dogs are intelligent animals, and they can learn incredibly quickly. They can be trained to do some amazing tasks, including loading and unloading the washing machine, turning lights on and off, and closing doors behind them. Some dogs are even trained to help their owners get dressed, go shopping, and use the ATM! Your dog may not need to learn these kinds of tasks, but he will need to learn basic manners. He should respond when you ask him to sit, lie down, and come when called. It's easy to train your dog when you know how—and your dog will love learning!

Think about what makes learning fun for you and your dog. You will need to be a patient teacher to help your dog succeed at his lessons and understand our language. Dogs love kind words, food treats, games, and affection, so be generous with your rewards and be thrilled when your dog does well! Once your dog has mastered the basic exercises, you may feel inspired to teach him some more advanced tricks—useful, clever, or just fun! Give them a try and challenge your dog's brain today!

**Your dog will need to learn good manners.**

# What dogs think about training

Dogs know how to sit. They also know how to lie down and perform hundreds of other behaviors. What they don't know is how to do these things on command. Some people try to make dogs obey them by shouting or being forceful, but this will just confuse the dog and will make her want to avoid her owner. To train your dog well, you must understand how she learns. You can use your knowledge to help her have fun learning new tasks.

Your dog will watch you to find out what you want.

Switching off your eye contact and body language tells your dog that you are no longer playing or training.

## Look and learn

Most dogs are visual learners. This means they watch us intently to see what we want. Although we like to tell dogs what to do by using our voices, many dogs will pick up on tiny body language signals from us that tell them what to do.

In one study, sheepdog handlers were asked to give their dogs commands, such as "sit" and "lie down." The dogs were very well trained and responded right away when they could clearly see their handlers. But when the handlers were asked to put on a pair of dark sunglasses and a hat, the dogs started to make mistakes! This is because dogs watch our facial expressions—even tiny movements of our eyes tell them what we want!

## LOOKING OR LISTENING?

Try this experiment to see if your dog is really listening to you, or whether she's "reading" your body language instead.

🐾 Stand facing a full-length mirror.

🐾 Call your dog to you.

🐾 Without turning around to look at her, ask her to sit.

🐾 Watch her in the mirror!

Does she sit immediately or does she look confused? Some dogs will try to walk around you, so that they can look at your face!

If your dog sits right away, she was listening to your voice. If she tries another option or walks away, chances are she needs to look at you to understand what you want.

## Make learning fun!

There's no doubt that when humans have fun, we learn better. The same goes for our best friends, too. Think about a time when you have really enjoyed learning something new dancing, swimming, skateboarding, or even math! Whatever the task was, your enjoyment probably made time fly. You probably had great fun and felt pride in your new ability. Maybe you even wanted to show off your new skill to others. Dogs are no different. Dogs that are enjoying training just can't get enough. They are often eager to show off their new behavior just for fun, too! Remember to take breaks from training every 10–15 minutes. You'll both find it difficult to concentrate if you get tired!

## Freedom at large

Training may help to keep your dog happy and occupied, but even more important, it will give her more freedom, too. A dog that's trained to be well-behaved in public and that walks nicely on the leash will be invited out more often than one that creates havoc! If she behaves, your dog will get more walks, and go out with you and your family more often than if she's a nuisance. Best of all, she will have more opportunities to run and play with other dogs.

**Walking nicely: Well-trained dogs have more fun!**

# Rewards, rewards, rewards!

**Everyone likes rewards for a job well done, and dogs are no different. Dogs need to know that good behavior gets rewards in the same way that we get a star for good work at school, or a treat for passing an exam. Using rewards encourages good behavior!**

## Why use rewards?

Quite simply, what gets rewarded gets repeated! If you want your dog to repeat a certain behavior, such as sitting, reward him and he'll do it more! Dogs are intelligent and quickly work out what's fun and what's not. Just like us, they avoid unpleasant experiences. This means that if you scold your dog or tell him off, he may simply avoid you in the future. Of course, to a dog, many things in life are rewarding. This is why some dogs behave in a naughty way. If your dog jumps up at the kitchen counter and discovers a delicious ham sandwich, chances are that he'll look there again the next day!

**Dogs can be trained to do amazing tricks!**

### DOG FACTS

🐾 Dogs can be trained to perform some amazing feats. Dogs can detect illnesses in people, can hunt for criminals, and can guide the blind.

🐾 Most dogs can learn a new behavior in just four tries if they are well rewarded for it.

🐾 Dogs can work out puzzles, like mazes. In fact, lots of dogs love to do this. Why not set one up in your own home?

**Fetch is a useful trick, and one that golden retrievers enjoy.**

More than anything, dogs love attention from us. They love us looking at them, talking to them, and touching them. This means that sometimes telling them off can have the opposite effect. The dog might repeat the naughty behavior to get more attention! Barking is a good example. If your dog barks and you shout at him, what do you think he hears? We think we are telling him off, but he thinks we are barking encouragement!

## TOP TIP

Many people think that giving a dog a pat on the head is a good reward. But to a dog this is just plain bad manners! Not many dogs like being patted on the head, and nearly all would choose a biscuit instead. Think about it from your own point of view: You get an A in a school exam. Which would you rather have as a reward—a pat on the head or a new bike?

## YOUR DOG'S REWARD CHECKLIST

Check off your dog's favorite type of reward in each category, and add any others you think of:

**Toys**

- [ ] Ball
- [ ] Tug toy
- [ ] Soccer ball
- [ ] Squeaky toy
- [ ] Soft toy

**Treats**

- [ ] Hot dogs
- [ ] Liver treats
- [ ] Cheese
- [ ] Dried dog food
- [ ] Dog biscuits

**Petting**

- [ ] Tickles on the chest
- [ ] Scratches on the rump
- [ ] Strokes on the back
- [ ] Tummy rubs

## What is a reward?

A good reward is anything your dog likes. In theory, you could use daily activities that your dog likes as rewards: going for a walk or being allowed to get on the couch. However, when you're training, you need to be able to give lots of small rewards in a short space of time. This means food treats are nearly always the best. Think about what food treats your dog would really love. Some dogs adore tiny bits of chopped hot dogs. Some dogs love store-bought treats. Others like healthy alternatives like small pieces of fruit or vegetables. If you are feeding your dog a dry dog food at mealtimes, then a handful of this usually works very well. Check with a parent that the type and amount of food you're using is appropriate.

**Food treats are useful tools in training.**

# Getting started

Starting to train your dog is easy. You just need a little space and a quiet time when you and your dog can both concentrate. Make sure you have your rewards in a container—small, soft, tasty treats are best—and you're ready to go!

**Training your dog to pay attention when you say her name is the most important part of her schooling.**

## Getting your dog's attention when you say her name

Getting your dog to look at you when you are indoors is easy, but attracting her attention when she's outside with a squirrel in her sights is another matter! You need to practice this exercise anywhere and everywhere.

**1** Stand in front of your dog. Say your dog's name in a happy voice.

**2** As soon as she looks at you, say "good" and give her a treat. The phrase "good" tells her what she's being rewarded for.

**3** Repeat this three or four times.

**4** Now practice when your dog is a little distracted—see if you can get her to whip around and look at you as soon as you say her name.

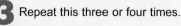

## Sit on command

Training your dog to sit on command is simple and very effective! There are hundreds of things your dog can't be doing when she's sitting. Just think! If your dog is sitting, she can't run away, jump up, chase things, steal shoes, chew your toys…The list is endless, so teach her to sit on command today!

**1** Show your dog you have a food treat in your hand. Put it close to her nose, so she can smell it.

**2** Lift your hand up and back, so she has to look right up to follow your fingers. This movement causes a physical chain reaction—her rear end has to go down. Be careful to keep your hand near your dog's nose. If your hand is too high, she will jump up to try and get the food.

**3** Say "good" and give your dog a reward as soon as she sits. Now say the word "sit" just before you move the food lure.

**4** Repeat this several times.

**5** Now you need to get your dog to sit without using food. Leave the treats in their container, so that you have no food in your hands.

**6** Ask your dog to sit, just once! If she does, say "good" immediately, then give a food treat from the container. If your dog does not sit when asked, help her by pretending that you have a treat in your hand, then say "good" and reward her for making an effort.

### "SIT" IS FUN

**North, south, east, and west**
Ask your dog to sit in front of you. Say "good" and reward her. Now move so you are facing a different direction, and ask her to sit again. Do this twice more so that she has sat facing all corners of the room!

**Smart sit**
Ask your dog to sit, then start counting the seconds until she does. If she does it in under three seconds, you throw the treat so that she can chase after it. Between three and five seconds and she gets a treat from your hand. Over five seconds means no treat at all!

**Test that sit!**
Ask your dog to sit. Now see if you can keep her sitting down while you bend your knees, clap your hands, or sit next to her on the floor. The ultimate test is to see if you can roll a ball past her without her standing up!

**Teach your dog to sit reliably on command in every situation.**

# Housebreaking

Dogs are naturally very clean creatures and will always choose to go to the toilet away from their den if possible. However, we still need to teach our dogs to be clean in the house and to give them plenty of opportunity to go to the toilet outside.

### Toilet matters!

Learning to predict when your dog needs to go to the toilet is the first step. The times when this is most likely are:

🐾 After he has eaten
🐾 After he has woken up
🐾 After a play session or any exciting event, such as you coming home from school

You also need to be able to spot the early warning signs that your dog needs to go out. Most dogs will sniff around on the floor, begin to circle or squat, or they may begin to appear distracted.

**1** When you suspect your dog needs to go to the toilet, encourage him outside with you. Take him to the same place each time, and give him a command, such as "Be quick!"

**2** Wait with your dog, then give enthusiastic praise, treats, or a game as soon as he has finished going to the toilet.

**3** After a few minutes, if your dog is showing no signs of going, take him back indoors. At this stage you know he is very likely to go soon. You must keep your eye on him the whole time to make sure he doesn't get the chance to make a mistake.

If you cannot supervise your pup, it's important to restrict him to a crate or an area that is easy to keep clean. Never scold or punish your dog if you let him make a mistake! It's just an accident.

### Housebreaking star chart

Stick gold stars on a calendar each time your puppy goes to the toilet in the right place. How many stars are there? The number of stars should increase every day!

**We must make sure we help our dogs learn how to be clean!**

## Puppy biting

Biting during play is normal for all young puppies under the age of 18 weeks, but you need to take action to stop it. Puppies have very sharp little teeth—when they bite, it hurts! This helps him discover what's alive and what's not.

Take all the fun out of biting for your puppy. Don't laugh, squeal, or shout if your pup bites. Instead, your puppy needs to know that biting hurts!

**1** Every time he mouths your hands or clothes, yelp loudly or give a big "Ouch!" or shout, then turn away as if to nurse your wounds.

**2** Ignore your pup for about 20 seconds, then continue touching him. Repeat the "ouch" and turn away each time you feel his teeth.

**3** Your puppy's biting should become more gentle over a period of about three to four weeks. At this point, your pup will realize that he cannot put any pressure on you. After this you can yelp even if he puts his mouth on you gently—finally teaching him that he cannot bite you at all.

# Lessons for life

**Although it may seem amazing, all our pet dogs are descended from wolves, and although they differ in many ways from their truly wild cousins, they have not lost all their similarities. Studies have shown that if dogs don't have enough contact with people when they are puppies, they grow up to behave as if they are wild. These dogs never learn to trust humans or to enjoy their company.**

Puppies learn how to be friendly with people during a very short period of their development: between 5 and 12 weeks of age. Of course, puppies do continue to learn after this time, but their whole outlook is likely to be affected by their experiences in this period.

## Meeting and greeting

Puppies need to meet and mix with as many different people as possible in order to feel confident in later life. To a puppy, a human being wearing a helmet may well look like a being from outer space, while children who have been to a carnival and had their faces painted must be totally unrecognizable!

All puppies need to be exposed to as many sights, smells, sounds, tastes, and touches as possible, in order to be able to cope with the world around them.

**TOP TIP**
If your puppy seems a little nervous when she meets something new, don't force her. Let her build confidence in her own time. Ignore her when she looks worried; praise and reward brave behavior instead.

**Pups need to meet as many different animals and people as possible.**

**Greet your puppy by crouching down.**

## Action plan for your puppy

As soon as your puppy is home, she needs to mix with as many people as possible and discover the world around her. Even if she hasn't completed her vaccinations, she can be carried out and about to see and hear traffic, baby strollers, and the general hustle and bustle of life. Bear in mind that puppies need to be exposed to many different kinds of environments, particularly those that you may visit in the future. This means that if you live in the countryside, trips to town will be vital. If you live in town, take a trip to the country!

### DOG FACT

Many puppies are carsick to begin with, but just like us, they grow out of it with time and practice. Short and frequent journeys in the car are essential for all puppies to get accustomed to the motion of the vehicle. Take your pup on the train or bus, too. The more she experiences now, the more confident she will be with different forms of travel later.

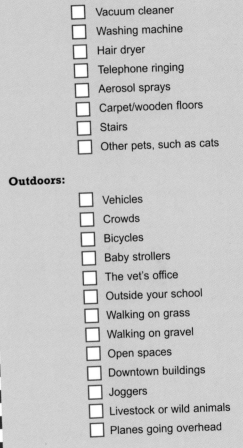

### BEEN THERE, DONE THAT!

Check the box when your puppy has seen and heard these things. Give her a gold star when she's seen and heard them three times or more!

**In the home:**

- [ ] Vacuum cleaner
- [ ] Washing machine
- [ ] Hair dryer
- [ ] Telephone ringing
- [ ] Aerosol sprays
- [ ] Carpet/wooden floors
- [ ] Stairs
- [ ] Other pets, such as cats

**Outdoors:**

- [ ] Vehicles
- [ ] Crowds
- [ ] Bicycles
- [ ] Baby strollers
- [ ] The vet's office
- [ ] Outside your school
- [ ] Walking on grass
- [ ] Walking on gravel
- [ ] Open spaces
- [ ] Downtown buildings
- [ ] Joggers
- [ ] Livestock or wild animals
- [ ] Planes going overhead

# Don't do that!

**Dogs are not always angelic! Sometimes they can behave in ways that we find annoying or even dangerous. When this happens, dogs are not usually being naughty for the sake of it. They are simply showing normal, natural behavior, which we may find difficult to live with.**

If your dog is doing something that you don't like, try to see the situation from his point of view. You will quickly see the problem from a whole different angle! For example, if your dog gets overexcited when your friends arrive, ask yourself whether they are accidentally rewarding him by getting excited themselves. If your dog seems too boisterous, ask yourself whether he is getting enough exercise outdoors, or if he's bored in the house. If you shout, maybe he thinks you are really barking encouragement! Try to "think dog" rather than getting annoyed. You'll be surprised at the difference it can make.

## Jump-free zone!

Jumping up is usually a friendly behavior, particularly in puppies, so it's important that we don't punish our dogs for doing it. Instead, think about what you would prefer your dog to do when greeting people—either keeping all four feet on the ground or, even better, sitting!

Teaching "sit to greet" is relatively simple:

**1** First make sure that all jumping up at home is ignored by your family.

**2** Turn your back and fold your arms if your dog jumps up; praise and pet if he is sitting or being calm.

**3** It's very important that no one strokes him when he's jumping up—no matter how pleased to see him they are!

**Turn away from your puppy if he jumps up.**

### TOP TIP
Many dogs love fetching a toy when you arrive home from school, and this seems to stop them from jumping up as well.

## Stealing the attention

Stealing items from around the house
and running off with them is a dog sport!
Unfortunately, it can lead to all sorts of
problems later on if it is encouraged at an
early age. Sporting dogs are especially likely
to discover that running off with your toys or
your headband gets the whole household in
an uproar. That's the equivalent of winning the
doggy lottery!

Again think about this behavior from your
dog's point of view. There he is, lying on the
carpet, being ignored. He chews gently on a
dog toy. Still, he is ignored. Bored, he gets up
and wanders over to your toys. He picks one
up. Suddenly, the whole household descends
on him! He runs away and a great game of
chase starts up around the house and yard!
Guess what he will do next time he wants to
have some fun!

## Stop your dog from stealing

Make sure that your dog can't get hold of
your most precious things. Puppies especially
love socks, hair scrunchies, pens, and shoes!
If your pup picks up something he should
not have, but you can sacrifice it, then do.
Dishcloths, washcloths, and tissues can all
be ignored. Just be sure your pup isn't eating
what he stole. Stand up and walk out of the
room to show you really don't mind.

Never shout or chase your puppy for the
item. Instead, call him to you, praise him, and
give him a treat in return for objects you can't
sacrifice. Work on teaching your dog to fetch
items for you (*see* page 73). This uses his
natural instincts and will keep him out of trouble!

**Dogs often steal to
get a reaction.**

# Lie down!

**Most dogs learn how to lie down when you ask, but they need motivation. Use a delicious food treat to help them at the start. Just like when you do math at school, dogs need time and patience to get it right!**

## Teach your dog to lie down

**1** With a food treat held close to your dog's nose, lower your hand slowly down to the floor, directly between her front paws. Hang on to the treat by turning your palm down, with the food hidden inside your hand. This way, the dog will want to burrow her nose underneath, and she will turn her head sideways to lick at it.

**2** You will be able to tell if your dog is trying—she will raise a paw to try and get the treat from your hand, her front end will go down in a bowing position, or she will move backward slightly. All these things mean you just have to wait. Eventually her whole body will flop to the floor.

**Lure your dog slowly into the down position by using a food treat.**

**3** The instant your dog lies down, say "good," then drop the treat onto the floor and let the dog eat it. This prevents the dog from following your hand back up again like a yo-yo!

**4** Repeat this several times, sometimes with the food in your hand, sometimes without. Once you can guarantee that your dog will lie down by following your hand to the floor, you can now say the word "down" just before you move your hand. Practice this at least 20 times!

## Without using food as a lure

**1** Now stand up straight. Show your pup that you have a food treat, then tuck your hand behind your back.

**2** Quietly ask your dog to "down," but don't help her with your hand. Most dogs will try sitting or even giving a paw before having the idea that lying down might work. Be patient and try not to repeat the word.

**3** The instant that your dog lies down, say "good," then give her several treats!

**4** Repeat this several times in several different places in the house and yard, until your dog is responding reliably anywhere and everywhere.

*Practice keeping
your dog in the
"down" position for
longer periods.*

## Now stay!

Once your dog has learned to sit or lie down on command, you can then teach her to stay in that position for longer, by waiting before you say "good" and treat.

**1** Ask your dog to sit or lie down, count to two, then say "good" and give the treat.

**2** Ask your dog to sit or lie down, wait five seconds, then say "good" and give the treat.

**3** Ask your dog to sit or lie down, wait seven seconds, then say "good" and give the treat.

**4** Ask your dog to sit or lie down, count to 30, then say "good" and give lots of treats!

## TRAINING GAME

Your challenge is to see if you can keep your dog lying down while you:

🐾 Tie your shoelace. *(Score two points)*

🐾 Stand still with your hands on your head! *(Score one point)*

🐾 Clap your hands! *(Score three points)*

🐾 Watch a commercial on TV. *(Score four points)*

🐾 Take two steps away and two steps back toward your dog. *(Score two points)*

🐾 Kneel on the ground next to your dog, then stand up again. *(Score three points)*

🐾 Hardest of all: Walk all the way around her! *(Score five points!)*

**How did you do?**

Add up all your points.
The highest score is 20.

*0–4 points*: Uh-oh! Go back to teaching your dog how to lie down on command and stay. Practice for a while, then try again!

*5–10*: Well done. Practice makes perfect. Have another try at the difficult ones!

*10–15*: Excellent! You've obviously done your homework. Go for 20 out of 20 next time!

*15–20*: Genius! You and your dog will go far. Keep up the good work!

*Put your hands on your hips.
Does your dog stay put?*

# Coming when called

Teaching your dog to come when called will give him more freedom when outside. However, make sure the area is safe for your dog to be off leash and that there is no traffic or other animals close by. Keep him on the leash if there is no adult with you to supervise.

## Starting out

**1** Standing only a couple of steps away from your dog in your home, call him in a friendly voice. For example, "Shadow, come!"

**2** Waggle the food treat in your outstretched hand to encourage your dog to come to you. If he doesn't respond, clap your hands or make silly noises. Then, using the food as a lure, move backward, just one or two paces. If your dog moves just one step toward you, say "good" and give him several treats right away by dropping them on the floor in front of you.

**3** Gradually increase the distance your dog has to come to get the food, making sure you praise him a lot. If your dog likes playing with toys, play a game as a reward sometimes, too.

**4** Now practice calling your dog to you at unusual moments in and around the house, then in the backyard. Build up your dog's recall before practicing in the park or woods, where there are more distractions. Here you can use a long or extending leash if you are unsure how your dog will respond. Bear in mind that the more distractions there are, the better your rewards and praise need to be!

Your dog should love coming when you call. Try to call him only for good things, like cuddles, food, and walks.

**TOP TIP**
Never scold your pup for taking too long to come to you—it will only discourage him from returning next time!

## Make outside fun!

Some dogs tend to be very good at coming when they are called because they know their owner is going to give them wonderful treats and games. Other dogs choose to be "conveniently deaf" in the park—probably because their owner ignores them until they are going to head for home! This teaches the dog that their owner is very boring compared to all the sights and smells around him, and also that coming when called means the end of his fun! Make sure you are fun to be with on a walk. Play with your dog often. Give him lots of rewards for coming to you during the walk, not just when you are going to put his leash on and take him home!

### RACING RECALLS

This is a good game to play with your whole family. The idea is to see who can get the dog to come to them the quickest. Your dog will tell you who he thinks gives the best praise and treats for coming when he's called.

🐾 Make sure each member of the family has the same number of food treats—say, 20.

🐾 Spread out so that you are about the same distance away from one another.

🐾 The first person calls the dog and everyone must now count to see how long the dog takes to reach them.

🐾 As soon as he comes, they say "good" and give him some treats. They decide how many depending on how quickly the dog came!

🐾 The next person then calls the dog—and tries to beat the first person's score.

🐾 Continue until everyone in the family has had two turns or until all the treats are gone!

**Your whole family can help your pup learn to come when he's called. Keep it fun and happy!**

# Walking on a leash

**The main reason so many dogs pull on the leash is that they get rewarded for it! By pulling, they get to the park more quickly, and lead their owners wherever they want to go, rather than the other way around!**

You need to start your dog's leash training in a calm, quiet place, not when you are trying to get to the park! Dogs need information about when they are in the right place when walking nicely on the leash, and this is where the word "good" as a signal really comes into its own. Rather than telling the dog off for pulling, take away all her fun by simply standing still. When the dog is in the right place, let her know by saying "good," giving a treat, then moving forward.

**All dogs need to be trained to walk nicely on a leash.**

## Lead the way!

1 Put your dog on the leash in the living room, hallway, or yard. Stand still to begin. Hold the leash close to your body to prevent your hand from being pulled toward the dog. Do not take a single step if the leash is tight.

2 Hold a food treat in your spare hand. Let her know that it's there! As soon as your dog puts slack in the leash and looks at you, say "good" and give a treat.

3 Walk just one or two steps in any direction you choose. Watch your dog's position carefully. If there is tension in the leash, stand still, or suddenly change direction. Do not walk in the direction your dog wants to go if the leash is tight!

4 Every time there's slack in the leash, say "good," and give a treat.

5 Repeat this several times, then stop and have a game. Be generous with the food to begin with—it's a difficult exercise for your dog!

Once your training indoors and in the yard is going well, you can begin to practice outside on walks. Don't expect too much too soon! You may stand still more than you walk forward at first, but be patient.

## The perfect collar and leash

What kind of collar and leash would your dog choose? To be safe and comfortable, dogs need a collar that is as wide as possible, and no less than ¾ inch in width. You should be able to put two fingers under the collar to check that it fits properly. Your dog's leash can be made of any material, such as leather or nylon, but chain leashes are uncomfortable to hold and can frighten your dog if you drop them accidentally.

**Head-collars are a way to stop your dog from pulling on the leash (right). They act like a halter on a horse and give you power steering. Harnesses are a comfortable alternative (above). Choke chains and prong collars should never be used. There's no substitute for good training and practice!**

Matching collars and leashes come in all different designs, colors, and patterns. You can even buy glamorous collars with gemstones or flashing lights for nighttime walks!

# Leaving food and objects

**Dogs explore the world by picking things up with their mouths to check how they taste and feel. They also steal for attention. Teaching your dog not to touch items can be a real lifesaver, as well as saving your toys from being chewed, too!**

To teach your dog the "leave" command, make sure you are somewhere calm and quiet. If your dog is greedy or uses his teeth, ask an adult to help you at the beginning.

**1** Hold a treat in your hand and close your fingers around it tightly. Hold your hand out to your dog and wait while he sniffs and licks, trying to get the food. Stay silent. Keep your hand still if you can.

**2** Hatch carefully. As soon as your dog takes his nose away from your hand, even for a split second, say "good," then give him the treat.

**3** Repeat this several times. Many dogs learn to take their mouth away from your hand in about four tries.

**4** Now you can wait until your dog has taken his nose away from your hand for the count of three, then say "good" and give a treat. Lots of dogs turn their face away completely as if to resist temptation. This is a good sign!

**5** Build up the amount of time that your dog will wait with his nose well away from your hand to about 10 seconds. At this point you can add in the command "leave." Say this in a calm, quiet voice, before the dog sees the food.

**6** Once your dog has gotten the hang of this, repeat the exercise, but this time say "leave," then show your dog the food on your open hand. If he tries to take it, close your fingers around the food. Do not snatch your hand away.

**7** Extend the exercise by practicing with food in your hand, on surfaces, and on the floor. Over a number of repetitions, dogs of all ages learn very rapidly that the word "leave" means "don't touch"—no matter what the item or where it is.

**Beware! Dogs are brilliant scavengers. If you leave food out unsupervised, they will eat it!**

When teaching "leave," hold a food treat tightly in your hand. Wait for your dog to take his nose away from it before rewarding him.

## Test your training

How good are your training skills? Don't forget to reward and praise your dog when he's done well.

| Task | Dog's response | | |
|------|----------------|------|----------------------|
|  | Excellent | Good | Needs more practice! |
| Ask your dog to sit four times in a row. | | | |
| Ask your dog to lie down, then watch a commercial on TV. Your dog must stay down the whole time! | | | |
| Walk your dog on a loose leash around the yard or up and down the driveway. No pulling allowed. | | | |
| Ask your dog to leave a piece of food on your open hand for a count of 10. | | | |
| Ask your dog to sit, then lie down, with no food in your hand. | | | |
| Ask your dog to sit. Put his leash on. He must remain sitting while it's clipped on and then taken off again. | | | |
| Call your dog to you from another room, using one command only. Does he come right away? | | | |

**Your results:**
*7 out of 7*: Excellent! Congratulations!
*4 out of 7 or more*: Well done. Keep up the good work!
*Less than 4 out of 7*: Needs more practice. Remember, all dogs work at their own pace.

# Tricks to amaze your friends!

**Tricks are a wonderful way to keep your dog amused and to build your relationship even more. From a dog's point of view, all exercises and tasks that you teach her are tricks, so keep it fun and lighthearted. Your dog will love it!**

## Roll over

Teaching your dog to roll over on command makes grooming easy and means that your dog is confident with you. It's also a great trick, especially if well practiced!

**1** Ask your dog to lie down.

**2** Once she is down, watch which way your dog's hips are angled. Using a food treat close to the side of your dog's mouth, lure her head so that she is looking backward, over her own shoulder.

**3** Follow through with the food treat, while the dog flops onto her side.

**4** Encourage your dog all the time. Keep a tight hold of the food treat while she rolls right over onto her back. Say "good," and give a treat as soon as she rolls right over.

**5** Stop luring your dog over as soon as possible. Let her work out what she has to do to get the "good" and treat.

**6** Add the phrase "roll over" only when your dog is doing it all on her own.

**7** Perfect the trick by practicing until your dog can dive into a roll over from a standing position, then stand back up again. This looks really impressive!

**Teaching your pup to roll over helps to build her confidence.**

Some breeds, such as Dobermans and whippets, find it difficult to perform this trick on hard surfaces, probably because they have rather bony, unprotected backs. Try practicing on a soft rug or blanket, and reward them for even the smallest effort in the right direction.

## Give a paw

A cute trick that looks as though your dog is shaking hands!

**1** First encourage your dog to sit in front of you. Give her a tiny piece of food from your hand.

**2** Hold another piece tightly in your clenched fist, close to the floor. Now watch carefully! You are going to say "good," then release the treat the instant your dog moves her paw. Most dogs will initially attempt to snuffle at the food with their noses or mouths. If you hold on to the food, she will then try a different tactic, by touching your hand with a paw. Reward her immediately. Repeat at least four times.

**3** Now make a rule. Your dog must make a deliberate move to touch your hand with her paw before getting the reward.

**4** Lift your hand a few inches from the floor. Your dog will have to reach higher to touch you with her paw. Say "good" and give a treat immediately for good attempts.

**5** At the point where your dog is reliably offering you her paw, you can add the command word. Say "paw" or "shake," then wait. It won't be long before your puppy is shaking hands on command!

Some breeds seem to be especially good at giving a paw on command. Golden retrievers, Labradors, and springer spaniels are often experts. Watch out if you have a glass of juice in your hand!

**Nice to meet you! Teach your pup to give a paw.**

# More tricks to amaze your friends!

## Spin

Teaching your dog to spin is a cute trick. Some dogs, such as collies and Jack Russell terriers, particularly love this trick. If you're a really good trainer, you can teach your dog to spin around on a doormat—so he wipes his own feet when he comes in from outside!

**1** Move a food treat in a big, wide circle to lure your dog around, so that his head nearly meets his tail. As soon as he's gone full circle, say "good," and give him a tasty treat.

**2** Repeat this several times until your dog starts to move around in a circle to follow your hand automatically.

**3** Now lure your dog around, but don't have a food treat in your hand. Say "good" and give him a treat if he spins the whole way. Be really pleased with him!

**4** Add the command. Say "spin" just before you start to move your hand. Practice this many times until your dog begins to move when you say the word.

**5** To make the trick look really professional, it's best if your dog responds to a word rather than a hand signal. Stand upright and ask your dog to "spin." If he does, say "good" and give him a whole handful of treats! He is a genius after all! If he hesitates for a while or looks confused, help him by making a tiny movement with your hand, then see if he can figure it out!

**Most dogs will happily follow a food treat into a spin. Move your hand slowly at first.**

## Figure eights

Teaching your dog to move in a figure eight around your legs takes skill—and balance! Take your time to teach this trick slowly and carefully, especially if you have a big dog or short legs.

**1** Stand still, holding a food treat in each hand.

**2** Starting with your dog on your left, bend your right knee forward and lure your dog through and under your right leg with the treat in your right hand. Say "good" and give him the treat.

**3** Repeat this several times, so that your dog is really confident at coming through and under your bent leg.

**4** Now repeat again, but instead of giving the treat after he's gone under your right leg, immediately show him that you have a treat in your left hand, too—behind your left knee. Lure him through and under your left leg, then say "good" and give him the treat.

**5** Put the two movements together. You will now find that your dog is doing a figure eight through your legs! Practice this stage lots of times and be generous with your treats and praise. Ignore your dog if he makes a mistake—instead just try again!

**As well as using food treats, give your dog plenty of praise and encouragement.**

After a while, practice the trick without food in your hands. Then start to prompt your dog by moving your knee rather than luring with your hands. Quick dogs can even weave in and out of your legs while you are walking along!

# Even more tricks to amaze your friends!

## Walk backward

A funny trick that also has its uses! Move your dog away from the TV, back her into a small space, or get her onto the scale at the vet's. It's good fun!

**1** Your dog needs to be standing in front of you. Hold a treat right up close to her nose so that she knows it's there, then move it down so that it's a little way under her chin.

**2** Most dogs will now take a small step backward to try and pop the treat into their mouths! Watch carefully. As soon as you see her back feet moving, say "good" and release the treat.

**3** Repeat this several times. It is quite difficult for some dogs to make the connection between thinking about their back paws and getting the treat, so be patient and make sure you say "good" clearly when you see her move back.

**4** Gradually increase the number of backward steps your dog has to take in order to get the reward. Practice a little and often, and make sure your dog is having fun! Say the word "back" to ask your dog to walk backward just before you move the treat under her chin.

**5** Finally, try the trick without a food treat in your hand. If your dog responds to your hand signal alone, then say "good" and give her several treats all at once. She deserves it!

**Hold a treat under your dog's chin and she'll step backward to get it.**

## Fetch

Some dogs, such as Labradors and spaniels, naturally retrieve items. Others need a little encouragement. This trick has many uses. If your dog will fetch, you can ask her to bring you letters, items of clothing such as socks, and even the TV remote control!

The art of a perfect retrieve is getting your dog to hold on to an item and then give it to you when you ask.

Always say "good" and give a treat in the early stages of teaching this exercise. However, after a while, the fun of playing chase games with toys will be rewarding enough!

**1** Start with a toy or an object that your dog likes, such as a soft toy or a piece of cloth.

**2** Have some tasty treats ready. Holding the object in your hand, offer it to your dog. If she even sniffs it, say "good," then give a treat. Repeat this a few times.

**3** Now wait for something a little more. This time you want your dog to try to take the object in her mouth. If she does, let her hold it for one second, then say "good" and treat. Build up the time she will hold the object to about 20 seconds.

**4** Now put the object on the floor. You can wiggle it and make it move like a snake, but don't throw it.

**5** As soon as your dog grabs hold of the toy, let it go, and immediately move backward. Encourage your dog to come to you and then ask her to give you the toy.

**Teaching your dog to retrieve has many benefits.**

# Stay safe around dogs you don't know

You may be an expert at understanding your own dog's behavior, but always be careful around dog "strangers." Just like people, some are friendly and others are not. Follow the guidelines below to make sure you keep safe.

## Steer clear

Never approach a dog that you don't know. Although a dog may look friendly, he may not want to play or be petted. Never, ever go near a dog that is out on its own, or groups of dogs that are roaming.

If a dog is with its owner, it is polite to ask before you pet it. If they say that you may, hold out your hand and let the dog sniff you before you touch him. It is canine bad manners to try to touch a dog on the head or neck. Most dogs prefer to be tickled on the chest. The owner will know that you understand dog behavior!

## Be a tree!

Never run away from a dog, scream, or wave your arms. This excites dogs, and may make them likely to chase you. Instead, act like a tree! Keep very still and fold your arms. Looking directly at a dog can be seen as a threat, so look away and wait for him to walk away. Call out to an adult if you are worried.

## Play it safe

Although it may be tempting, never play with any dog unless an adult is with you. Even small dogs can be strong and very fast, and may hurt you without meaning to. Big dogs might knock you over accidentally, so always have an adult with you if you are having a game with a dog.

**Stay still and calm if you are unsure about a dog you don't know.**

*Some dogs can't resist bikes. Use yours as a barrier if you feel worried.*

## Dog danger!

Never, ever approach a dog that is tied up or attached to a chain, or tease a dog behind a fence or gate. These are very dangerous situations, so keep clear. Mother dogs caring for puppies may also be upset if you approach, so ask an adult before touching.

## Cycle alert

Some dogs are very excited by seeing children on bicycles. They want to run and chase. The faster you pedal, the more they want to catch up. If a dog you don't know approaches you when you're on your bike, the best way to deal with it is to get off. Stand still with the bike between you and the dog. Keep quiet, stay still, and wait until the dog loses interest before wheeling your bike away, or call out to an adult to help you.

## Let sleeping dogs lie

This is a great expression! Never disturb a dog that is sleeping, as you may surprise him. Just like us, some dogs can be very grumpy when they are woken up suddenly!

## Don't take my food!

Dogs that are eating or chewing on a bone or toy may feel threatened if you are too close, so give them a wide berth. Never try to take something away from a dog's mouth—even if you think the dog might hurt itself.

## TOP TIPS

🐾 Never approach a dog you don't know!

🐾 Always ask the owner before touching their dog.

🐾 Never tease dogs, scream, or run away from them.

🐾 Ask an adult for help if you are worried.

# Games and Fun

**Dogs love to play games. Chase, tag, hide-and-seek, and treasure hunts are all on their list of favorites! Games are important to dogs for many reasons: They help to build friendships, they allow the dog to practice "hunting" skills, and they are a great way to let off steam!**

In the wild, a dog would have to spend a large amount of his day searching for food—hunting for it, finding it, and eating it. He would have to be good at digging for roots and finding berries and fruit. He would need to search for water to drink and would have to find a good place to sleep, too. In our world, dogs have far less to do. They are given food to eat from a dish, are taken for a walk when we decide, and have water on tap! Although this gives them an easier life, it can also make them bored and a bit frustrated, too. Some may get into mischief if we don't give them enough to do and to think about. Games and puzzles give your dog a way to use his natural abilities and exercise his brain, too. How many can you invent?

**Games are important to dogs for many reasons.**

# Puzzles and games

Your dog comes equipped with special searching and puzzle-solving equipment—her eyes, nose, and brain! Dogs are designed to find food, shelter, and playmates in the wild. It's no wonder they get bored just sitting next to the sofa. Playing games that allow your dog to use her special skills will give her an outlet for her energy, and she'll want to be with you more than ever.

## TREASURE HUNT
Perfect for: Active dogs who love their toys.

**You will need:**
- 🐾 Your dog's favorite toy

**Rules of the game:**
- 🐾 Ask your dog to sit and wait while you hide her toy in another room.
- 🐾 Go back to her and tell her to go find the toy.
- 🐾 Go with her and encourage her to seek it out.
- 🐾 If your dog is good at this game, hide the toy in more difficult places each time!

## SCATTER SEARCH
Perfect for: When you're short on time!

**You will need:**
- 🐾 Your dog's dinner
- 🐾 A backyard
- 🐾 A Kong (a rubber pyramid toy with a hole inside)

**Rules of the game:**
If you feed dry food and have access to a yard:
- 🐾 Ask your dog to sit and wait while you throw her food out onto the grass.
- 🐾 Tell her to go find—and eat!

If you feed a wet food (such as canned food):
- 🐾 Ask your dog to sit and wait while you squash her food into a Kong toy using a spoon.
- 🐾 She must then work at the Kong to get the food out.

**Dogs are excellent at finding hidden objects, so make this her favorite game!**

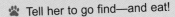

## MUG SHOTS

Perfect for: Clever dogs who like a challenge.

**You will need:**
- Some treats
- An old cup or mug
- A watch with a second hand or a stopwatch

**Rules of the game:**
- Ask your dog to sit while you place a food treat under the upturned mug.
- Tell her to find the treat, and then time how long it takes her to get it.

All dogs have different ways of approaching this puzzle! Some will use their paws to push or knock the mug; others will use their nose or teeth to move it. Some smartie-paws will even pick up the mug by the handle to get at the food!

Once your dog has solved this puzzle, repeat it and time her again. Is she quicker the second, third, and fourth times?

## MESSAGE IN A BOTTLE

Perfect for: Dogs who like to figure things out.

**You will need:**
- Some bits of your dog's dry food or some dry treats
- A large empty water bottle (throw away the lid and test that it crumples without splitting)

**Rules of the game:**
- With your dog sitting by your side, pop the treats into the empty bottle.
- Give your dog the bottle and let her work out how to get the treats out by shaking and rolling it!

**Keep your pup's brain busy and active.**

# Playing with toys

**Play is a very important part of your dog's life. It is thought that play helps a puppy's brain to develop, as well as allowing him to have fun and practice hunting skills!**

Some dogs are very excited to play and will chase toys and tug them naturally. Others need a little help and encouragement.

Follow the guidelines below to ensure that your dog plays by the rules!

**1** Always use a toy! Don't allow your dog to mouth your hands, clothes, or hair, or to wrestle on the floor. Use a long tug toy, a ball on a rope, or another toy that keeps your hands well away from your dog's mouth.

**2** Teach your dog to tug by holding the toy low to the ground and moving it like a snake along the floor. Allow your pup to chase the toy, then pounce on it and grab it. Have a gentle tug game!

**3** Now teach your dog to drop the toy when you ask. After a tug game, keep your hand on the toy, but don't put any pressure against it. Now offer your dog a really tasty treat to eat. It's impossible for him to keep the toy in his mouth and eat the food at the same time, so as soon as he drops the toy, say "good" and let him eat the food. Leave the toy where it is—don't whisk it away or your dog will think you are a toy snatcher!

**4** As soon as your dog has eaten the food, play again and repeat the routine. After three or four tries, most dogs will drop the toy voluntarily when they see the food coming. As soon as this starts to happen, say "drop" or "give" very quietly, just before he lets go.

**5** Your dog must abide by the golden rules of play. If he so much as touches your hand or skin with his teeth while playing, you say "too bad," and the game finishes that instant!

**Keep toys low to the floor when playing, and teach your dog to let go on command!**

## Playing solo

Dogs need to learn to occupy themselves when they haven't got company. This doesn't include raiding the garbage or chewing the furniture! Chew toys and toys that reward lone play are perfect alternatives.

Kong toys or hollow toys like activity balls, which can be filled with food, are good. Old cardboard boxes and empty water bottles make great playthings, too, especially if you put a couple of pieces of dry food inside them! Test that the plastic bottle crumples without splitting.

## Two-toy magic

If your dog is good at chasing toys but wants to play keep-away rather than bring them back to you, try this trick to make sure you always have one toy each!

## BEST TOYS FOR YOUR DOG

To play with you:
- 🐾 Tug toys
- 🐾 Balls on ropes
- 🐾 Balls for throwing
- 🐾 Soccer balls

To play with by himself:
- 🐾 Kongs
- 🐾 Chews
- 🐾 Buster cubes
- 🐾 Activity balls
- 🐾 Safe empty water bottles

**1** Start with two identical toys. Throw one for your dog and let him chase it, then bring it back. Don't try to take the one he has, but instead throw your toy up in the air and play with it yourself. Your dog will soon lose interest in the one he has and will want yours instead!

**2** As soon as he drops his toy, you can throw yours, and then pick up the other one. This keeps your fingers safe and you in control of the game!

**Use two identical toys if you want to stay in control of the game.**

# Outdoor pursuits

## On the right track

Dogs use their noses a lot! As humans, we can only guess how much information dogs pick up through their sense of smell. Your dog's natural ability to use her nose can be channeled by taking part in tracking and searching.

Either a scent is laid for your dog to follow or articles are left along a trail for your dog to find. This is an activity any breed can take part in—you don't have to own a bloodhound! It's wonderful to watch your dog following an "invisible" trail and doing something that comes so naturally to her.

Tracking is something you can do yourself, or you can join an organized group. If you want to try it yourself, start out by finding an area of grass—the yard or a park—that hasn't been walked on for a few hours. You may need to get up early for this!

All dogs have a great sense of smell and can be taught to follow a track outdoors.

**1** Tie your dog up safely, or ask someone to hold her for you.

**2** Start at a certain point, such as next to a tree, or put a stick in the ground so you know where your starting point is.

**3** Walk 10 paces in a straight line, away from the starting point. After 10 paces, stop, and place some food treats in a pot or place your dog's favorite toy on the ground.

**4** Walk back along the same path that you took.

**5** Now get your dog and take her to the starting point. Encourage her to sniff the ground by showing her with your hand. Allow her to follow your trail and then give her the reward at the end!

**6** Practice teaching your dog to follow longer and longer trails every day. She'll soon become an expert at tracking you, your friends and family, or even pretend "criminals" like a police dog!

## Doggy dribbler

Most dogs love to play soccer! Some breeds will push the ball with their noses, some will use their paws, and some just love being the goalie. Have some food treats and a soccer ball ready.

**1** Ask your dog to sit, so that she is concentrating.

**2** Place a treat right under the ball, and allow your dog to find it. She will push the ball out of the way with her nose in order to get to the treat. Say "good" as soon as her nose touches the ball.

**3** Practice this about 10 times. Pick the ball up in between each go.

**4** Now place the ball down, but don't put a treat underneath. Most dogs will push it anyway to see if there's some food there. Say "good," and give her a treat from your hand if she does. Practice this game lots of times until your dog is dribbling the ball like a pro!

**Bend it like Beckham! Is your dog the next great soccer star?**

# Sports and events

Having fun with your dog can be a great way of making new friends and learning new skills. There are lots of clubs and activities associated with dog sports, and lots of these encourage young people to join in. Some even run summer camps for kids and their dogs!

## Agility for all!

Joining your local dog agility club is a great way for your dog to get fit and make new friends, too! Your dog will learn to jump hurdles, run through tunnels, and walk along high beams—a bit like show jumping for dogs. Any breed can have a try, but your dog does need to be more than a year old to take part in jumping.

## Flyball fun

Flyball is a fast and furious game that is based on a relay race between dogs. Dogs must run in a straight line away from their owner, jump over four hurdles, trigger a special box to release a tennis ball, catch the ball, and then run back over the four hurdles and "hand over" to the next dog in their team. Phew! Any breed or size of dog can take part, as the height of the hurdles reflects the smallest dog in the team. Why not give it a try?

**Dogs love jumping! Your dog will need to be more than one year old and healthy to join an agility club.**

## Working trials

Working trials were developed to test the working ability of dogs like German shepherds. Dogs learn to track and search for missing objects, negotiate high jumps and long jumps, walk to heel, retrieve a dumbbell, come when called, stay when told, and be sent away from the owner to a particular spot. Training for this sport requires lots of practice and often involves being out in all weather. It's definitely for outdoor types!

## Swim along

All dogs can swim, although some breeds are better at it than others. Breeds such as the Newfoundland, poodle, and Portuguese water dog were bred to work in and around water. If you don't have the sea or a lake nearby, don't despair. Doggy swimming pools are the answer! Some pools even let you swim with your dog.

## Dance party

Dancing with your dog, also known as "heel work to music," is great fun! Dogs are taught to perform tricks while moving to the music, and handlers often dress up to match the theme of the tune they're dancing to. If you have taught your clever dog a few tricks, why not put them together and perform them to a song that you like for your family and friends? Your dog will love the applause!

**Dancing with dogs is becoming a popular sport.**

### MAKE A MINI OBSTACLE COURSE

You can make a mini obstacle course in your own backyard.

- 🐾 Make mini hurdles from bamboo canes balanced on empty water bottles. Choose the height according to your dog's size.
- 🐾 Construct a "dog walk" from a plank of wood, balanced on bricks. Put the brick in the middle to make a mini seesaw!
- 🐾 Secure a play tunnel to the ground (to prevent rolling). These are available from toy stores and make a great birthday present for you or your dog.

# Questions you've always wanted to ask!

### Does my dog dream?

It's very likely that dogs dream when they are asleep. Some dogs may growl, whine, or twitch while they're sleeping, as if they're running or snarling. Of course, we don't really know whether dogs dream in pictures and sounds in the same way we do, but it certainly seems like dogs can have the equivalent of nightmares, as well as pleasant dreams, from the way their bodies move in their sleep!

A Chihuahua (left) and a Great Dane (right): Dogs are incredibly diverse in their personalities, their shapes, and of course their size!

### Why does my dog yawn?

Dogs yawn for lots of different reasons—not just because they are tired! People and dogs both yawn when they are stressed out, bored, or feeling relieved. Yawning allows the dog to take in more oxygen, which means his body will be ready for action, but it also allows the muscles to relax. Yawning is highly contagious. You may even feel like yawning while you are reading this! Dogs often "catch" yawning from one another, and may even copy us when we do it, too!

### What is the smallest breed of dog?

The Chihuahua is the smallest breed of dog. They may weigh as little as 2 pounds, and as puppies they can fit in your hand! The tallest breeds of dogs are the Irish wolfhound, Great Dane, Saint Bernard, borzoi, Anatolian Karabash, and the English mastiff. They can get to be 35 inches at their shoulders.

## Can my dog see color?

Of course, we can't ask dogs what they can see, and this makes it difficult to know exactly how they view the world. We do know that dogs' eyes are made quite differently from human eyes, and that they don't have the same number or type of cells that allow us to see color. But their world is not black and white. Although they probably can't see reds or greens, they can see other tones and shades of color to some extent.

Dogs have far better night vision than us. This means they can see objects in the dark as if they are glowing. Dogs are also able to detect movement much better than humans, and it's thought they can see flickering light better than us. This might mean that dogs see pictures on the television as a series of snapshots rather than a moving image!

**It is thought that dogs circle before they settle down as a kind of nesting behavior.**

## DOG FACTS

🐾 The oldest dog on record was 29 years old. He was an Australian cattle dog.

🐾 The basenji is the only breed of dog that doesn't bark. Instead, they make a sound like a yodel!

🐾 Dalmatians are born white. Their spots only begin to develop when they are about two weeks old.

## Why does my dog circle before she settles down to sleep?

Dogs often circle around and around before they settle down. It is thought that this behavior is a kind of nesting. In the wild, a dog would settle down to sleep outdoors on leaves and moss, not indoors in a comfy bed. Our pet dogs still have the instinct to make their beds as cozy as possible. Walking around in a circle tramples the bedding into a perfect nest shape!

# Why does my dog...?

**Dogs have impressive teeth for tearing, biting, and grinding their food.**

## Why does my dog have such big teeth?

Dogs are omnivores. This means they eat both meat and vegetables. In the wild, dogs would have to hunt for their dinner—chasing, catching, and killing their prey. Their large front canine teeth are hooked like fangs to allow them to grip prey and tear flesh. Whereas our back teeth are shaped for chewing, theirs are shaped for grinding up bones and muscle. Dogs' teeth are like formidable weapons—and they carry them around all the time! Thankfully, when dogs are puppies, they learn how to use their mouths in a gentle way. This makes it safe for us to be around them.

**Licking is a sign of affection that begins between puppies and their mothers.**

## Why does my dog lick me?

Dogs lick people as a sign of affection. This starts when dogs are puppies and are licked clean by their mother, which feels comfortable and reassuring. Puppies also lick their mother to show that they want food. By licking around her mouth, they hope that she will regurgitate some food for them. This action is never forgotten, and some dogs lick their human owners to show their affection for years after they are tiny puppies. Licking is also a dog's way of gaining information about people and their surroundings. Dogs have a very good sense of smell and they sometimes taste things at the same time to enhance this. Some breeds of dog seem to lick more than others. Flat-coated retrievers, for example, are well known for the amount of licking that they like to do!

## Why does my dog growl when we play?

Dogs growl for lots of different reasons. They may make this sound when they are frightened or as a warning for us to keep away. However, dogs will also growl when they are playing, pretending to be fierce as a part of mock fighting. Maybe this is a bit like playing "monsters" with your friends in the playground! Dogs most often growl if they are playing with a toy and are tugging on it in a battle of strength. On the whole, growling during play is nothing to be worried about, as long as the rest of your dog's body language looks relaxed and friendly. If your dog shows his teeth, suddenly goes still, or puts his teeth on you while playing, then stop immediately.

## Why does my dog walk past other dogs in a curved line?

Dogs are very good at greeting each other politely when out for a walk. If both dogs are off the leash, chances are one of them will walk in a wide curve around the other, before they have a sniff to say hello. This is a bit like introducing themselves and is far friendlier than walking at each other head-on, which might be interpreted as a threat. Walking in a curve gives each dog a little time to assess the other and means that they can feel reassured by the other dog's polite behavior.

Dogs greet each other in a polite
and friendly way by approaching
in a curve rather than head-on.

## DOG FACT

Dogs have two sets of teeth, just like people. The first set, known as deciduous teeth, is the equivalent of baby teeth. These become loose and gradually fall out by the time the puppy is about five months of age. You may find some of these teeth on the floor after your puppy has been chewing or playing.

# Glossary

**Adolescence** The period, from around 5—18 months of age, in which your dog is the equivalent of a human teenager.

**Agility course** A doggy obstacle course, including jumps, tunnels, and raised walkways.

**Body language** A dog's use of body postures, facial expressions, and tail wagging to communicate.

**Canine** A word that is used to describe all things doggy, which comes from the Latin term for "dog," *Canus*.

**Chew or chew toy** A toy especially designed to chew, such as a rubber bone.

**Command** The word you say when you want your dog to move into a particular position, e.g. "sit," or perform a task, e.g. "fetch."

**Crate** An indoor kennel for your dog (right).

**Crossbreed** A mixture of two well-known breeds of dog.

**Grooming** Brushing, combing, nail clipping, and tooth brushing for your dog.

**Sporting dogs** A type of dog that traditionally went out on hunts to retrieve fallen birds, e.g., golden retrievers and cocker spaniels.

**Headcollar** Very similar to a horse's bridle. Instead of a collar that goes around the neck, the headcollar fits over the dog's muzzle and head instead.

**Herding and "pastoral" breeds** Dogs used on farms to help herd sheep, cows, and sometimes other animals, such as geese! An example is the border collie.

**Hounds** Dog breeds that went out on hunts to help spot the prey and track it. They might have excellent eyesight and be able to see things a long way off, like the greyhound; or have great noses for following scents, like the bloodhound.

**Kong** A hollow, rubber toy for your dog to chew on, which can be stuffed with treats.

**Littermates** A dog's brothers and sisters.

**Lure** To use a tidbit to encourage your dog into the position you want her to be in.

**Mongrel or mutt** A mixture of many different breeds or types of dog.

**Muzzle** A dog's nose and mouth.

**Play bow** When the front end of your dog is down, but her bottom stays up in the air, she is play bowing to invite you or another dog to play.

**Reward** Anything your dog likes in return for doing something good; usually a food treat, or a game with a toy.

**Socialization** Introducing your dog to lots of other dogs and people, so that she gets used to communicating with them.

**Terrier** Dog breeds associated with work on the ground or underground, chasing rats or rabbits for example, e.g. the Jack Russell terrier.

**Toy dogs** The name for a group of breeds, usually small, that love companionship and cuddles on your lap, e.g. Cavalier King Charles spaniels and Yorkshire terriers.

**Tracking** When a dog uses her nose to follow a scent trail left behind by a human or another animal.

**Trail** A series of signs left behind by a person or animal. We cannot see a trail, but our dog can smell it.

**Treat** A small piece of food that your dog likes, such as hot dog.

**Tug toy** A toy that can have a dog on one end and a human being on the other! A tug toy might be a knotted rope or a ball on a rope.

**Wet/dry food** Wet dog food comes in cans. Dry dog food is in pellets and often comes in a box or sack.

**Working and utility breeds** These dogs traditionally performed all sorts of tasks to help humans. Some were guard dogs, like the Doberman, and some helped out on the farm, like the Bernese mountain dog, which pulled carts.

**Vet** An animal doctor.

# Web sites

**www.aspca.org/animaland**
American Society for the Prevention of
Cruelty to Animals (ASPCA) Animaland—
for kids who love animals.

**www.akc.org/kids_juniors/**
American Kennel Club—Kids and
Juniors section.

**www.bestfriends.org/theanimals/
petcare/dogs**
Dog-specific advice from the Best Friends
Animal Sanctuary in the United States.

**www.thekennelclub.org.uk**
The Kennel Club U.K. site features helpful
information about dog ownership.

**www.dogtrain.co.uk**
Sarah Whitehead's United Kingdom-based
training site. You can download useful fact
sheets in the "Quick Bites" section.

**Talk to your
friends who also
have dogs and
exchange ideas.**

# Organizations

## United States and Canada

### American Kennel Club
260 Madison Avenue
New York, NY 10016
Tel: (212) 696-8200
www.akc.org

### American Society for the Prevention of Cruelty to Animals (ASPCA)
424 East 92nd Street
New York, NY 10128-6804
Tel: (212) 876-7700
www.aspca.org

### Best Friends Animal Society
5001 Angel Canyon Road
Kanab, UT 84741-5001
Tel: (435) 644-2001
www.bestfriends.org

### The Canadian Kennel Club
89 Skyway Avenue, Suite 100
Etobicoke, Ontario, Canada M9W 6R4
Tel: (416) 675-5511
www.ckc.ca

## United Kingdom

### The Kennel Club
1 Clarges Street
London W1J 8AB
Tel: 0870 606 6750
www.the-kennel-club.org.uk

### The Pet Advisory Committee
1 Bedford Avenue
London WC1B 3AU
Tel: 020 7255 5489
www.petadvisory.org.uk

## Australia and New Zealand

The Australian National Kennel Council lists organizations by territory. Visit their website—www.ankc.aust.com—if your local group isn't listed below:

### Dogs New South Wales (NSW)
PO Box 632
St Marys NSW 1790
Tel: (02) 9834 3022
or 1300 728 022 (NSW only)
www.dogsnsw.org.au

### New Zealand Kennel Club
Prosser Street
Private Bag 50903
Porirua 6220
Tel: (04) 237 4489
www.nzkc.org.nz

# Index

# Acknowledgments

## Photography

Jane Burton and Kim Taylor (Warren
Photographic): 1, 2, 7l, 8, 9, 12m, 13, 20r, 21l,
22, 23, 25l, 26tm, m, mb, 28l, 32r, 33, 35r, 37,
39, 40b, 43l, 44tl, 44tr, 45tl, 45tr, 52r, 54, 55,
56tl, 59, 63tl, bl, 64, 65br, 68t, 76, 77, 81t, 84b,
90l, 93; Corbis: 42r, 86t; David King: 27rb; J.L.
Klein & M.L. Hubert (Oxford Scientific Films):
16l; Andrew Sydenham: 18l, 80t.